THE HANUMAN CONSCIOUSNESS

The Alchemy of Strength and Surrender

Kanav Sachdev

White Light Publication

THE HANUMAN CONSCIOUSNESS
The Alchemy of Strength and Surrender

White Light Publishers Gurgaon, Haryana

ISBN-13: 978-81-996899-2-3 (Ebook)
ISBN-13: 978-81-997518-4-2 (paperback)
ISBN-13: 978-81-996899-5-4 (Hardcover)
ISBN-13: 978-81-997518-6-6 (Audio)

Cover design by: Jyoti Sachdeva

To the Jambavan in your life, the one who saw the divine fire in you when you saw only doubt.

To the Vayu-Putra within you, the one who is infinitely strong, eternally devoted, and perpetually free.

May the words in these pages be the Shravanam that breaks the curse of amnesia, not just for you, but for every soul you touch.

May you remember your true lineage. May you fortify your vessel. And above all, may you leap in service.

CONTENTS

Title Page
Copyright
Dedication
Introduction
Author's Note
Disclaimer
Chapter 1: The Jambavan Effect 1
Chapter 2: The Biology of Power 18
Chapter 3: The Breath of the Father 34
Chapter 4: The Leap of Faith 51
Chapter 5: Monsters in the Deep 64
Chapter 6: The Spy in the Citadel 75
Chapter 7: The Ring of Remembrance 96
Chapter 8: Controlled Chaos 104
Chapter 9: The Sanjeevani Mindset 120
Chapter 10: The Humble Victor 132
Chapter 11: The Open Heart 140
Conclusion 154
Glossary of Sanskrit Terms 155
THE COMPLETE LIBRARY OF KANAV SACHDEV 157
About The Author 171

INTRODUCTION

The Sleeping God Within

There is a moment in every life that feels like the edge of the world. You stand before a challenge—a crisis, a dream, a calling—that seems too vast to cross. The data says it is impossible. Your logic says you are unqualified. You look at the distance between where you are and where you need to be, and you feel a distinct shrinking of the spirit.

In the corporate world, they call this "Imposter Syndrome." In psychology, it is "Learned Helplessness." But in the ancient spiritual tradition of the Ramayana, this paralysis has a specific name. It is the silence of Hanuman.

We are accustomed to thinking of Hanuman as the god of unassailable strength—the one who lifts mountains as if they were pebbles, the one who leaps across oceans as if they were puddles. We worship the result, but we ignore the process. We forget that before he was the Leaper, he was the Forgotten. Before he was the hero, he was the doubter who sat on the sands of the southern ocean, convinced of his own insignificance.

This book is not about worshipping a deity outside of you. It is about accessing a frequency inside of you. The "Hanuman Consciousness" is not a religious concept; it is a psychological state. It is the state of total integration where the primal strength of the animal meets the infinite devotion of the saint. It is the alchemy of turning Force into Service.

In the pages that follow, we will deconstruct the Sundara Kanda and the Yuddha Kanda not as mythology, but as a manual for high performance and spiritual awakening. We will look at the science of energy management (Brahmacharya), the psychology of resilience (Titiksha), and the art of extreme ownership.

You are not a broken vessel. You are a sleeping god. You have simply forgotten who your Father is. It is time to remember.

Kanv Sachdev 2026

AUTHOR'S NOTE

A Message from the Heart

To the Seeker holding this book,

You have picked up the first volume of a journey designed to map the architecture of your own soul. This book, The Hanuman Consciousness, is the foundation. It deals with the body, the breath, and the capacity for action. It is the "Earth" on which the rest of the spiritual structure will stand.

Why This Book Is Required We live in an age of paralysis. We have more information than ever before, yet we are frozen by doubt, "imposter syndrome," and a profound sense of weakness. We have forgotten our own strength. We are like Hanuman sitting on the beach, unaware that we can fly. I wrote this book to be your "Jambavan"—the mirror that reminds you of who you are. This text is not just about a monkey god; it is about the physics of devotion and the biology of power. It is required because without a strong container (the body/mind), the spiritual energy we seek will only shatter us.
An Apology to the Divine To Lord Hanuman, the Son of the Wind and the Breath of the World: I bow to You. You are beyond words, beyond intellect, and beyond the tiny grasp of my pen. If I have simplified Your glory, if I have misrepresented Your power, or if I have failed to capture the subtlety of Your devotion, I ask for Your forgiveness. My intention was not to define You, but to point towards You. May the reader look past my limitations and feel Your presence in the space between the words.

How to Use This Book This is a manual for high performance.

Read Actively:

Do not just read the chapters; test them. When we discuss the "Victory Log," grab a pen and write. When we discuss "Breath," stop and breathe.

Do the Work: The "Sadhana" sections are non-negotiable. Information without application is just spiritual obesity. You must metabolize these truths through action.

Start Small: Hanuman did not start by lifting the mountain; he started by serving Rama. Start with the small disciplines of the body (diet, sleep, celibacy/moderation) before attempting the great leaps of the mind.

What to Expect Expect to feel uncomfortable. This book will ask you to confront your laziness, your excuses, and your smallness. But also expect to feel a surge of energy you haven't felt in years. Expect to remember that you are not a victim of your circumstances, but a servant of the Highest Truth. Expect to find your wings.

In Service and Strength,

Kanv Sachdev

DISCLAIMER

Please read this disclaimer carefully before using this book or applying any of the principles described herein.

Fictionalization and Privacy

The case studies, anecdotes, and personal stories presented within this book are included for educational and illustrative purposes only. While they are inspired by real-world concepts and experiences, they are fictionalized. In all instances, the names, identifying details, professions, locations, and other key details of individuals have been altered or entirely fabricated to protect privacy and ensure anonymity. Any resemblance to actual persons, living or dead, or actual events is purely coincidental.

Not Professional Advice

The content of the book is intended to provide information, spiritual concepts, and personal development principles based on the author's interpretation of ancient texts and practices. It is not intended to be a substitute for professional medical advice, diagnosis, or treatment.

- Consult a Professional: Always seek the advice of your physician or other qualified health provider with any questions you may have regarding a medical condition or before undertaking any new breathing or physical practice, particularly those involving breath retention or physical implements (such as the Yoga Danda).

- Use at Your Own Risk: The practices described in this book should be approached with respect and caution. The author and publisher are not responsible for any adverse effects or consequences resulting from the use of any suggestions, practices, or preparations mentioned in this book. Your engagement with the material is entirely at your own risk.

CHAPTER 1: THE JAMBAVAN EFFECT

1.1 The Amnesia of the Soul (The Curse)

There is a moment in the spiritual journey where you find yourself standing on the edge of a precipice. The ground behind you is the life you have known—safe, predictable, and ultimately confining. The space ahead of you is a void—an ocean of uncertainty that demands a version of yourself you have not yet met.

You look at the distance between where you are and where you need to be, and you feel a distinct shrinking of the spirit. The mind, usually so adept at categorization and control, suddenly falls silent, not in peace, but in paralysis.

In the corporate world, they call this "Imposter Syndrome." In psychology, it is "Learned Helplessness." But in the ancient, rhythmic language of the *Ramayana*, this paralysis has a specific name and a specific mechanism. It is the silence of Hanuman.

We are accustomed to thinking of Hanuman as the deity of unassailable strength—the *Bajrangbali* (he whose limbs are as hard as the thunderbolt), the one who lifts mountains as if they were pebbles, the one who leaps across oceans as if they were puddles. We worship the result, but we often ignore the process. We forget that before he was the Leaper, he was the Forgotten. Before he was the hero who burned Lanka, he was the doubter who sat on the sands of the southern ocean, convinced of his own insignificance.

This chapter is not about how to acquire strength. You do not need to acquire what you already possess. The ocean does not need to acquire wetness; the fire does not need to learn how to burn. This chapter is about why you have forgotten that strength, and the specific spiritual "curse" that keeps the modern mind trapped in a loop of mediocrity.

The Myth Of The Empty Vessel

There is a pervasive lie in modern self-development that you are a "work in progress," an empty vessel that must be filled with skills, habits, and hacks to become valuable. This is the path of accumulation. It suggests that you are fundamentally insufficient, and through the hard labor of acquiring knowledge and status, you might one day become enough.

The Vedic vision, however, is radically different. It posits that you are *Purnam*—complete. You are born with the totality of the universe encoded in your subtle body. The strength of the wind, the stability of the earth, and the clarity of space are not external qualities to be bought; they are internal frequencies to be tuned into.

So, if we are born full, why do we feel so empty? If we are born as lions, why do we live as sheep?

The answer lies in the story of Hanuman's childhood, a narrative that serves as a perfect metaphor for the human condition.

The Child Who Ate The Sun

The scriptures tell us that Hanuman was born to Anjana and Kesari, but his spiritual father was Vayu, the Wind God. As a child, he was not just energetic; he was energy itself. He was *Virya* (vitality) uncontainable.

One morning, the infant Hanuman looked up at the sky and saw the rising sun. To his innocent, non-dual mind, the sun was not a distant star of burning hydrogen; it was a ripe, glowing fruit. Driven by the primal hunger of the spirit, he leaped.

This was not a jump; it was a defiance of gravity. He traversed the atmosphere, approaching the solar orb, threatening to consume the very source of cosmic light. The gods were terrified. Indra, the King of Heaven, fearing the disruption of the cosmic order, struck the child with his thunderbolt (*Vajra*). Hanuman fell, his jaw (*Hanu*) broken, his consciousness dimmed.

But the true tragedy was not the fall. It was what happened next. The Rishis (sages), annoyed by his unbounded, disruptive power, placed a curious curse upon him. They did not strip him of his strength—that would be impossible, for energy cannot be destroyed. Instead, they stripped him of his *awareness* of it.

They pronounced: *"O Monkey, you possess infinite speed and power, but because you use it without wisdom, you shall forget it. You will remain unaware of your own glory. You will live as a simple forest dweller, oblivious to the divinity that pulses in your veins, until the day someone reminds you of who you truly are."*

Pause here. Close your eyes and let this image settle in the heart space.

This "curse" is not a punishment inflicted on a mythological monkey thousands of years ago. It is the precise description of what has happened to you.

The Architecture Of Forgetting

We are all born as children of Vayu. Watch a child at play. They have boundless energy, an imagination that knows no physics, and a heart that loves without transaction. They are, in a sense, trying to eat the sun—trying to consume the whole world with their curiosity.

But then, the "Rishis" of our world intervene. The first Rishi is the educational system that tells you to sit still, to color within the lines, to memorize rather than imagine. The second Rishi is the family dynamic that says, "Be realistic," "Don't aim too high," "Who do you think you are?" The third Rishi is society, which values compliance over creativity and safety over sovereignty.

Slowly, layer by layer, the curse takes hold. We stop leaping at the sun. We start bargaining with gravity. We internalize the limitations placed upon us until we no longer need the external voice to stop us; we stop ourselves.

This is the spiritual definition of *Maya*. In popular Hinduism, Maya is translated as "illusion," as if the world is a hologram. But in the context of the Hanuman Consciousness, Maya is not illusion; it is *Amnesia*. It is the "Curse of the Rishis" operating in real-time.

It is the mechanism that makes a lion believe it is a sheep. It is the dust that covers the mirror, convincing the mirror that it has no ability to reflect light.

The Scene At Mahendra Parvat

Fast forward many years in the Ramayana. The infant who leaped at the sun is now an adult warrior. He is part of the search party sent to find Sita. They have reached the southern tip of the continent—Mahendra Parvat.

The situation is dire. The ocean lies before them, a vast, terrifying expanse of 100 Yojanas. To cross it is impossible for a normal being. To turn back is to fail Rama.

The Vanara army is in a state of collective panic. They are huddling together, discussing their constraints. Angada says, "I am the leader, but I am too heavy." Jambavan says, "I am too old."

Others offer small distances, negotiating with their mediocrity.

And amidst this noise, where is Hanuman? He is sitting apart, in the shadows, silent.

This silence is profound. It is not the silence of a sage in *Samadhi*; it is the silence of a soul in *Sushupti* (deep sleep). He is looking at his hands and seeing only fur and bone. He is looking at the ocean and seeing a barrier. He genuinely believes he cannot do it. The curse is fully active.

This is the state of the modern human. You stand before your own oceans—the business you want to start, the book you want to write, the trauma you want to heal. You know, deep down, that there is a power within you capable of the leap. You feel the stirrings of *Vayu* in your breath. But the mind immediately overlays the memory of past failures.

I am not smart enough. I am too old. I do not have the resources.

You sit in the corner of your own life, waiting. You are waiting for permission. You are waiting for a certificate. You are waiting for the stars to align. But the stars do not move for those who sit.

The Trap of the "Subjective Loop"

Why can't Hanuman just "snap out of it"? Why can't he just look in the mirror and see his muscles?

This brings us to a critical psychological insight: You cannot see the picture when you are in the frame.

When you are trapped in the "Subjective Loop" of your own mind, you are analyzing your potential using the very instrument that is malfunctioning. Your mind is the database of your past, and your past is a record of your limitations. You cannot use the past to calculate your future potential, because the future demands a version of you that the past has never seen.

Hanuman is trying to calculate the trajectory of the leap using the logic of a land-dwelling monkey. The math doesn't work. It will never work.

The curse ensures that the subject (you) cannot objectify its own power. The eye can see the whole world, but it cannot see itself. To see itself, it needs a reflection.

The Necessity Of Friction

The universe is designed in a way that potential energy requires friction to become kinetic energy. A matchstick is full of fire, but it is cold to the touch. It can sit in a box for a hundred years, holding an inferno within its wooden body, yet never burning. It needs the strike. It needs the friction of the rough surface to wake up the fire.

Hanuman is the matchstick. The curse is the box. He needs the strike.

This is why the spiritual path is rarely a smooth ascent. It is almost always a series of crises. The crisis—the ocean, the deadline, the heartbreak, the failure—is not an obstacle; it is the rough surface against which the soul is struck.

If the ocean were not there, Hanuman would never have needed to fly. If the crisis were not insurmountable, you would never need to access the "Zero Point" of your potential.

We spend our lives trying to avoid the oceans. We pray for bridges. We pray for boats. We pray for ease. But the prayer of the Hanuman Consciousness is different. We do not pray for the ocean to shrink. We pray for the back to strengthen. We do not ask for the removal of the obstacle. We ask for the removal of the amnesia.

The Waiting

So, here we stand at the end of this first movement. The ocean is roaring. The army is panicking. The hero is sleeping.

You are Hanuman. The ocean is your life's calling. The panic is your mind's chatter. And the silence? That is the waiting.

You are waiting for the voice that will break the spell. You are waiting for the "Jambavan Effect." But before we meet Jambavan, we must understand that the waiting is not passive. It is pregnant. The silence before the leap is not empty; it is gathering.

In the next section, we will turn our gaze from the sleeping monkey to the wise bear. We will explore the mechanism of the awakening—how the external voice penetrates the internal wall, and why, in the economy of grace, you sometimes need to borrow someone else's belief in you until your own belief catches up.

The curse is real. But so is the cure. And the cure begins not with a movement of the body, but with a movement of the ear. We must learn to listen.

1.2 The Mirror of the Mentor (Jambavan's Role)

There is a fundamental paradox in the human design: You cannot tickle yourself.

Try it. Run your fingers along your own ribs. The sensation is there, but the reaction—the convulsion, the laughter, the shock—is missing. Why? Because the brain anticipates the touch. It knows the source is you, and therefore, it cancels out the surprise. The feedback loop is closed.

This biological quirk points to a deeper spiritual truth: You cannot wake yourself up. If you are dreaming, the "you" in the dream is part of the dream. You cannot use the dream-self to exit the dream. You need an alarm clock. You need a shake. You need a voice from the outside.

This is why the self-help industry often fails. It is an attempt to tickle oneself. It is the ego trying to fix the ego using the tools of the ego. It is a closed loop. To break the curse of amnesia, we need an intervention. We need a force that stands outside our subjective reality and disrupts it. We need a Jambavan.

The Old Bear In The Shadows

In the *Kishkindha Kanda*, Jambavan is described not as a warrior in his prime, but as the King of the Bears—ancient, slow, and wise. He is the oldest member of the expedition. He has seen the Vamana Avatar of Vishnu; he has seen the churning of the ocean. He is the Keeper of Memory in a group of forgetful youth.

While the other monkeys are running around in panic, Jambavan observes. He sees Hanuman sitting in his silence. Jambavan does not see a monkey. He sees a dormant volcano.

He approaches Hanuman. The text implies a sense of reverence in his approach. He does not scold Hanuman for being lazy. He does not give him a lecture on "positive thinking." He simply holds up a mirror.

"O Hanuman," he begins. *"Why are you silent? Do you not know who you are?"*

This question—*Do you not know who you are?*—is the chisel that cracks the hard shell of the ego. Jambavan proceeds to narrate Hanuman's lineage. He speaks of Vayu, the Wind God. He speaks of Anjana, the celestial nymph. He speaks of the leap at the sun. He connects the confused, finite individual (Hanuman) back to his infinite source (Vayu).

He essentially says: *"The limitation you feel is real for your body, but it is a lie for your spirit. You are identifying with the container, not the content."*

The Pygmalion Effect

Modern psychology calls this the Pygmalion Effect (or the Rosenthal Effect). It is the phenomenon where higher expectations placed upon individuals lead to an increase in performance.

In a famous study, teachers were told that certain students in their class were "bloomers"—geniuses waiting to happen. In reality, these students were chosen at random. Yet, at the end of the year, those specific students showed a massive increase in IQ. Why? Because the teachers *looked* at them differently. They spoke to them with more patience. They held space for their genius to emerge. The belief of the teacher became the reality of the student.

Jambavan is the ultimate Pygmalion. Hanuman had zero belief in himself. The curse had wiped his hard drive. But Jambavan held the belief *for* him. Jambavan acted as an external hard drive where Hanuman's greatness was stored until he was ready to download it again.

This is the role of the Guru in the Vedic tradition. The word *Guru* is often mistranslated as "teacher." But a teacher gives you information you didn't have. A Guru takes away the ignorance you shouldn't have. *Gu* means darkness. *Ru* means remover. The Guru is not a master you worship; the Guru is a mirror you look into. When you look into a dirty mirror, you see a dirty face. When you look into the clear eyes of a mentor who sees your potential, you see your own divinity reflected back.

The Biology Of Belief

What happens physiologically when a Jambavan speaks to us?

The Ramayana gives us a graphic description. As Jambavan speaks, Hanuman begins to grow.

- "His form expanded like the ocean in high tide."
- "He roared like a lion, shaking the caves of Mahendra Parvat."
- "His tail lashed the ground, cracking the earth."

This is not just poetry; it is somatic reality. When you are trapped in "Imposter Syndrome," your posture collapses. Your breath becomes shallow (chest breathing). Your neurochemistry is dominated by cortisol and norepinephrine—the chemicals of fear and freeze. You are physically small.

But when you receive high-quality validation—when a mentor says, "I see you. You can do this"—the chemistry flips. Dopamine floods the system (motivation). Serotonin rises (status/confidence). Testosterone increases (action-taking). You physically take up more space. You stand taller. Your voice drops an octave.

Jambavan didn't inject Hanuman with steroids. He injected him with Truth. And Truth, when fully accepted by the nervous system, is anabolic. It builds you up.

The Tragedy Of Isolation

The most dangerous aspect of the modern world is not its noise, but its isolation. We have built a society that worships independence. We say, "I don't need anyone." We wear our loneliness like a badge of honor.

But in the spiritual physics of the Hanuman Consciousness, isolation is the incubator of the curse. When you are alone, your inner critic has no opposition. The voice that says "You are not enough" echoes off the walls of your skull, amplifying itself until it becomes the only truth you know.

Hanuman could have sat on that beach for a thousand years.

Without Jambavan, he would have remained a monkey. This is a hard pill for the ego to swallow. We want to be self-made heroes. We want to be the "Chosen One" who wakes up simply because we are special. But even God incarnate as a Vanara needed a wake-up call.

If Hanuman needed a Jambavan, who are we to think we can do it alone?

Who Is Your Jambavan?

This brings us to the first actionable audit of this book. Look at the circle of people around you. Most of us are surrounded by Angadas. Angada is the prince who said, "I can't do it, and if I do, I will die." Angadas are the people who share your doubts. They bond with you over trauma. They validate your victimhood. "Yes, life is hard. Yes, the economy is bad. Yes, we are just monkeys." Angadas feel safe because they demand nothing of you.

But do you have a Jambavan? A Jambavan is uncomfortable. He disturbs your sleep. He refuses to buy your excuses. He looks at your "limitations" and calls them lies. He might be a coach, a spiritual teacher, a demanding boss, or an honest friend. He is the one who remembers your "Leap at the Sun" even when you have forgotten it.

You cannot tickle yourself. You cannot bless yourself. You cannot initiate yourself.

You need the Other. The awakening of the Hanuman Consciousness begins with the humility to admit that your current view of yourself is incomplete, and the willingness to let someone else's vision of you override your own.

As Jambavan's words washed over him, the silence of the monkey was replaced by the roar of the god. The curse began to crack. But the transformation was not just psychological. It was vibrational.

1.3 *The Physics of Sound and Cell (Shravanam)*

We have established that the "Jambavan Effect" is the psychological trigger for awakening. But we must now go deeper. We must ask: *How* did a few sentences from an old bear cause a monkey to physically expand to the size of a mountain?

Was it magic? Was it poetic exaggeration? Or was it a demonstration of a fundamental law of physics that we are only now beginning to understand?

In the Vedic tradition, the universe is not made of matter; it is made of Sound (*Nada*). The first element is *Akasha* (Space), and the quality of Space is Sound (*Shabda*). Everything you see—from the granite of the mountain to the neurons firing in your brain—is condensed vibration.

When Jambavan speaks to Hanuman, he is not just conveying information. He is transmitting a frequency. This is the ancient science of *Shravanam*—the yoga of deep listening.

The Architecture Of The Ear

The ear is the most primitive and the most sophisticated sense organ. It is the first sense to develop in the womb and the last to leave at the moment of death. You can close your eyes, you can close your mouth, you can hold your breath, but you cannot close your ears. You are always open to vibration.

Hanuman, sitting on the sands, had closed his eyes in despair. He had closed his mouth in silence. But his ears were open. This was his saving grace.

As Jambavan's voice entered Hanuman's auditory canal, it bypassed the conscious, critical mind—the "Monkey Mind" that says *I can't*—and went straight to the cellular memory.

- "You are Vayu Putra."
- "You are the carrier of the Thunderbolt."
- "You are the servant of Rama."

These words acted like a specific code entered into a computer terminal. The code unlocked the dormant energy within Hanuman's DNA.

Cymatics: The Shape Of Sound

To understand this, look at the science of Cymatics. If you place sand on a metal plate and play a violin bow against the side, the sand rearranges itself into perfect, geometric mandalas. The chaotic grains of sand do not "choose" to become organized; the frequency *forces* them into order.

Your body is 70% water. Dr. Masaru Emoto's experiments famously demonstrated that water exposed to words of love and truth freezes into beautiful, symmetrical crystals, while water exposed to hate and doubt freezes into chaotic, ugly blobs.

Hanuman's body—his blood, his lymph, his marrow—was vibrating at the frequency of "I am small" (Chaos). Jambavan's voice introduced the frequency of "You are Infinite" (Order). Because Jambavan spoke with absolute conviction (Truth/Satya), his vibration was stronger than Hanuman's. The result? The "water" in Hanuman's body reorganized itself. The "sand" on the plate shifted. His physical expansion was simply his biology aligning with the new frequency.

This brings us to a terrifying and empowering realization: Your biology is eavesdropping on your biography. Every word you speak about yourself, and every word you allow others to speak into you, is physically restructuring your nervous system.

Shravanam: The First Act Of Yoga

In the path of Bhakti (Devotion), the very first step is not service (*Seva*) or prayer (*Vandanam*). It is *Shravanam*—hearing. Why? because you cannot serve what you do not know, and you cannot know what you have not heard.

Hanuman had to *hear* his glory before he could *live* it. But here is the nuance: *Shravanam* is not passive hearing. It is not the background noise of a podcast while you do the dishes. *Shravanam* is "drinking through the ears." It is an act of total surrender where you allow the sound vibration to enter your heart space and rearrange your furniture.

Most of us listen to reply. Or we listen to judge. Hanuman listened to receive. He became a vacuum. He emptied himself of his small identity so that Jambavan could pour the large identity in.

The Danger Of Toxic Sound

If sound can heal, sound can also kill. If Jambavan's voice expanded Hanuman, imagine what the voice of a toxic cynic does to you. When you surround yourself with "Angadas"—people who vibrate at the frequency of fear, gossip, and limitation—your cells entrain to that frequency. You physically shrink. Your cortisol spikes. Your immunity drops. Your "Ojas" (vitality) leaks out.

You would never drink poison if someone handed it to you in a cup. Yet, we drink verbal poison every day in the form of news, toxic social media, and cynical friends. To awaken the Hanuman Consciousness, you must become a guardian of your ear-gates. You must ruthlessly filter the frequencies you allow into your system.

1.4 Sadhana: The Victory Log (Pratipaksha Bhavana)

We have understood the myth, the psychology, and the physics. Now, we must move to the practice (*Sadhana*). How do you trigger the Jambavan Effect when you are alone in your apartment, far from the beaches of Kishkindha?

Here are three specific practices to break the amnesia of the soul.

Practice 1: The Victory Log (Likhita Japa Of The Self)

The brain has a "Negativity Bias." It is like Velcro for bad experiences and Teflon for good ones. You remember the one insult from ten years ago, but you forget the hundred compliments you received last week. This is why you feel small. You need to externalize your data.

The Protocol:

1. Buy a dedicated physical notebook. Do not use your phone. The act of writing engages the reticular activating system (RAS) in the brain.
2. Sit in a quiet space. Close your eyes. Take three deep breaths.
3. Write the title: "The Resume of Glories."
4. List 3 to 5 moments in your life where you faced an "Ocean"—a situation that felt impossible—and you crossed it.
   - *Example: The time I navigated that breakup without losing my dignity.*
   - *Example: The time I learned that software from scratch in two weeks.*
   - *Example: The time I stood up for myself against authority.*
5. Crucial Step: Do not just list the event. Write down *what quality* within you made it possible. Was it resilience? Was it patience? Was it stubbornness?

Why this works: When you read this log, you are playing the role of Jambavan for yourself. You are forcing your brain to look at the evidence of your own power. You are wiping the dust off the mirror.

Practice 2: Curating Your Council (Satsang)

If you cannot find a living Jambavan, you must find a digital or literary one.

The Audit:

- List the 5 people you text most often.
- Place a (+) next to their name if they energize you (Jambavan).
- Place a (-) next to their name if they drain you (Angada).
- Your goal is not to "cut off" everyone, but to consciously limit your exposure to the (-) and increase your exposure to the (+).

The Digital Jambavan: If your physical environment is barren, plug into the great minds. Listen to biographies of great beings. When you listen to the story of a Master, you are undergoing *Shravanam*. Their vibration temporarily overlays your own.

- *Action:* For the next 7 days, commit to 20 minutes of listening to high-vibration content (scripture, biography, or high-level philosophy) immediately upon waking. Do not check email or news first. Let the first sound that enters your ear be the sound of strength.

Practice 3: Pratipaksha Bhavana (The Counter-Thought)

Patanjali, in the Yoga Sutras (2.33), gives us the ultimate tool for negative thinking: *Vitarka Badhane Pratipaksha Bhavanam.*

"When disturbed by negative thoughts, cultivate the opposite mental attitude."

When the thought comes: *"I am too weak to handle this."* Do not fight the thought. Do not argue with it. Instead, immediately introduce the "Jambavan Thought." Use a *Mantra* or an Affirmation that anchors you to your source.

- *The Hanuman Mantra:* "Om Hum Hanumate Namaha" (I bow to the Prana within).
- *The Affirmation:* "I am the Instrument. The Doer is infinite."

The Micro-Practice: Whenever you feel the "Shrink" (the physical sensation of fear/doubt):

1. Stop moving.
2. Inhale deeply, expanding the chest (mimicking Hanuman's growth).
3. Exhale slowly.
4. Say audibly: *"This challenge is real, but my potential is greater. I have crossed oceans before."*

The journey of a thousand miles begins not with a step, but with a remembrance. Hanuman is awake. The bear has spoken. The dust is wiped from the mirror. But waking up is only the beginning. Now that the engine is running, we must ensure the fuel tank is full. We must ensure the vessel is strong enough to hold this awakened energy without cracking.

In the next chapter, we descend from the mind into the body. We will explore the lost science of *Brahmacharya*—not as moral repression, but as the physics of energy conservation. You have remembered you are a lion. Now, you must learn to hunt.

CHAPTER 2: THE BIOLOGY OF POWER

2.1 The Leaking Vessel (The Modern Crisis)

If Chapter 1 was about the awakening of the mind, Chapter 2 is about the fortification of the vessel. It is useless to wake up a lion if the lion is too weak to hunt. It is useless to remember you are Hanuman if your physical nervous system is too fragile to hold the voltage of that realization.

We live in an age of exhaustion. Look around you. We have more comfort, better nutrition, and more advanced healthcare than any generation in history. Yet, we are tired. We wake up tired. We rely on caffeine to simulate energy and alcohol to simulate relaxation. We are a species of high ambition but low vitality.

In the Vedic tradition, this state is called *Prana-Kshaya*—the depletion of life force. We are like clay pots filled with water, but the pots are riddled with cracks. No matter how much sleep we get, or how many "productivity hacks" we employ, the energy leaks out as fast as it enters.

To understand the Hanuman Consciousness, we must first understand the physics of this leak. Why was Hanuman the strongest being in the universe? It was not just because of his divine parentage. It was because he was a *Naishtika Brahmachari* —a being who never leaked his vital essence. He was a perfectly sealed vessel.

The Dopamine Loop

The modern leak is not just physical; it is sensory. The ancient Yogis understood a fundamental law of thermodynamics that modern neuroscience is only now confirming: Where attention goes, energy flows.

Every time you scroll through social media, every time you engage in compulsive pleasure-seeking, every time you fragment your attention across ten different tabs, you are bleeding *Prana*. The sensory organs (*Indriyas*) are described in the Upanishads as horses pulling the chariot of the body. If the horses are wild and uncontrolled, they drag the chariot into the ditch.

Today, we live in a "Dopamine Casino." The screen offers cheap, instant rewards—likes, notifications, pornographic images, sensational news. These are high-stimulation, low-satisfaction inputs. They spike your dopamine (anticipation) but drain your serotonin (contentment). The result is a nervous system that is wired and tired. You are over-stimulated but under-energized.

Hanuman represents the anti-thesis of this state. He is *Jitendriya* —the conqueror of the senses. He is not a repressed ascetic hiding in a cave; he is a warrior standing in the middle of Lanka (a city of gold and pleasure) without being consumed by it. He moves through the world of sensation without letting the world enter him.

The Physics Of Prana

Let us look at this through the lens of physics. Energy cannot be created or destroyed, only transformed. The energy you use to digest a heavy meal, the energy you use to argue with a stranger on the internet, the energy you use for sexual release, and the energy you use for spiritual creativity are all the *same* energy. It is all *Prana.*

The average human spends 90% of their Prana on basic maintenance: digestion, stress response, and sexual expulsion. There is nothing left for the higher functions—intuition, will power (*Sankalpa*), and spiritual perception. We are trying to launch a rocket, but we are using all our fuel just to keep the engines idling on the launchpad.

The "Leaking Vessel" cannot hold the "Zero State." You can meditate for an hour a day, but if you spend the other 23 hours leaking energy through your eyes, ears, and tongue, the meditation will feel dry. It will be like pouring water into a bucket with no bottom.

The Myth Of The Golden Deer

In the Ramayana, the trouble begins when Sita gets distracted by the Golden Deer. The deer is *Maya*—an illusion. It looks beautiful, but it is a demon in disguise. We are constantly chasing Golden Deers. We chase the perfect job, the perfect partner, the perfect body, thinking, *"Once I get that, I will be full."* But the chase itself drains us.

Hanuman never chases the deer. He chases only Rama. This is the secret of his power. His energy is single-pointed (*Ekagrata*). Because he wants only One Thing, he has infinite energy for that One Thing. Because we want ten thousand things, our energy is divided by ten thousand.

The Audit Of The Vessel

Before we can rebuild the vessel, we must find the cracks. Close your eyes for a moment. Bring your awareness into the body.

Where do you feel the leak?

- The Eye Gate: Do you consume visual junk? Do you watch violence or pornography that leaves a residue in the mind?
- The Tongue Gate: do you eat food that is dead (processed, heavy) or alive (*Sattvic*)? Do you speak words that are true, or do you leak energy through gossip and complaint?
- The Sexual Gate: Do you use sexuality as a drug to numb anxiety, or as a sacred exchange?

This is not a moral audit. The universe does not judge you. Gravity does not judge you if you jump off a cliff; it simply pulls you down. Similarly, the laws of Prana do not judge you. But if you violate them, the result is inevitable: weakness, brain fog, and spiritual amnesia.

To hold the Hanuman Consciousness, we must plug the leaks. We must begin the process of *Pratyahara*—conscious withdrawal of the senses. This brings us to the most controversial and powerful tool in the yogic arsenal: the conservation of sexual energy.

2.2 The Alchemy of Ojas (Virya to Tejas)

We now arrive at the core of the biological argument. In the West, sexuality is seen primarily as a biological function for reproduction or recreation. To suggest "holding it in" is often viewed as repression, leading to neurosis. Freud famously argued that suppressed libido leads to pathology.

But the Yogic science of *Brahmacharya* is not about suppression. Suppression is when you want it but say no out of guilt. That creates a civil war inside the body. *Brahmacharya* is about Transmutation. It is the alchemical process of turning a raw biological fluid into a subtle spiritual light.

The Seven Tissues (Sapta Dhatu)

To understand this, we must look at the Ayurvedic map of human physiology. Ayurveda describes seven layers of tissue (*Dhatus*) that are formed sequentially from the food we eat.

1. Rasa (Plasma): The first extract of digested food.
2. Rakta (Blood): The life-giving red fluid.
3. Mamsa (Muscle): The flesh and structure.
4. Meda (Fat): Lubrication and protection.
5. Asthi (Bone): The hard structure.
6. Majja (Marrow/Nerve): The filling of the bone and nervous tissue.
7. Shukra (Reproductive Tissue): The final, most refined essence.

It takes roughly 30 days and immense metabolic fire (*Agni*) to transform food into *Shukra*. Think of *Shukra* (semen in men, vital fluid in women) as the "Cash" of the body. It is the most concentrated form of energy you possess. It is potent enough to create a new life. It carries the code of your ancestry and the spark of consciousness.

When this fluid is released, the body must work overtime to reproduce it. It taxes the bone marrow, the blood, and the digestion. But if this fluid is *not* released—and here is the secret—it does not just sit there. If it is heated by the fire of Tapas (discipline) and Pranayama (breath), it undergoes one final transformation. It becomes Ojas.

What Is Ojas?

Ojas is the subtle glue that holds the consciousness to the body. It is the spiritual immunity. When you see a great saint or a high-performance athlete who seems to glow, who has a magnetic presence that fills the room, you are seeing *Ojas*. It is the gold produced by the alchemist.

Hanuman is the embodiment of *Ojas*. Because he is a *Brahmachari*, every drop of his vital potential is converted into spiritual radiance (*Tejas*). This is why he is invincible. An enemy can strike his body, but they cannot penetrate his aura, because his aura is thick with Ojas.

In the modern world, we are *Ojas*-deficient. We are "dry." Our eyes lack luster. Our skin is dull. Our minds are brittle. Why? Because we spend our "Cash" (Shukra) as soon as we earn it. We are biological spendthrifts.

The Hydraulic Metaphor

Imagine a hydraulic system. If you want to lift a heavy car, you need immense pressure. Sexual energy is the hydraulic pressure of the soul. If the pressure is constantly released through the safety valve (sex), the system never builds enough pressure to lift the consciousness to the higher centers (Chakras).

The goal of *Brahmacharya* is to build the pressure. Yes, this pressure can feel intense. It can manifest as agitation, anger, or intense desire. This is where most people fail. They feel the pressure and immediately release it to get "relief." But the Yogi says: "Hold the pressure." Do not release it. Steer it. Use that pressure to push the consciousness upward. Use it to fuel your focus, your work, your meditation.

Virya To Tejas: The Conversion

How does this conversion happen? It happens through Heat. Just as water turns to steam when boiled, sexual fluid turns to Ojas when boiled by *Tapas* (discipline).

This is why Hanuman is often depicted as red or orange—the color of fire. He is burning. Every time you feel the urge and *choose* not to release it, but instead channel it into a workout, a creative project, or deep breathing, you are heating the cauldron. You are churning the ocean.

This is not easy. The biology wants to reproduce. The DNA is selfish; it only cares about survival, not enlightenment. You are fighting millions of years of evolutionary programming. But this fight is the only war worth waging.

The Zero Point Of Desire

In my own practice of "Zero," I have found that desire is not the enemy. Desire is simply energy seeking a home. When you feel lust, do not judge it. Do not say, "I am bad." Simply witness it. Say to yourself: *"This is raw power. This is the same energy that created the stars. I will not waste it. I will keep it. I will let it rise."*

In the next section, we will look at the specific mechanism of this rising—the path of *Urdhvareta*. We will discuss the spinal dynamics and how the breath acts as the elevator for this potent energy. You are not a leaking vessel. You are a reactor vessel. And it is time to start the reaction.

2.3 Urdhvareta: The Upward Stream

We have spoken of the "Leaking Vessel" and the "Alchemy of Ojas." Now, we must speak of the mechanism. How exactly does one take a biological fluid, which is designed by nature to flow *down* and *out* for reproduction, and force it to flow *up* and *in* for evolution?

This process is called Urdhvareta.

- *Urdhva* means "upward."
- *Retas* means "stream" or "vital fluid."

In the ordinary human (the *Bhogi*), the stream of energy flows downward. It moves from the brain, down the spine, and exits through the genitals in search of pleasure or procreation. This is the path of *Pravritti* (outward engagement). It is natural, it is biological, but it is entropic. It leads to the dissipation of the self into the world.

In the Yogi (the *Hanuman*), the stream is reversed. This is the path of *Nivritti* (inward return). The energy is generated in the root, but instead of exiting, it is pulled upward through the spinal column (*Sushumna Nadi*), piercing the energetic centers (*Chakras*), until it reaches the brain (*Sahasrara*). When the vital fluid reaches the brain, it is not semen or hormones anymore. It becomes *Amrita*—the Nectar of Immortality.

The Physics Of The Spinal Column

To understand Urdhvareta, you must understand the "spiritual plumbing" of the human body. The spine is not just a stack of bones; it is a hollow tube designed to conduct high-voltage consciousness.

Inside the spinal column, there are three primary channels (Nadis):

1. Ida (The Moon): The left channel. It carries cooling, mental, feminine energy. It controls the parasympathetic nervous system (rest and digest).
2. Pingala (The Sun): The right channel. It carries heating, physical, masculine energy. It controls the sympa-

thetic nervous system (fight or flight).
3. Sushumna (The Void): The central channel. This is the "Zero" channel.

In most people, the energy alternates between Ida and Pingala. We are either too mental/passive (Ida) or too physical/aggressive (Pingala). The central channel remains dormant, closed like a blocked pipe. *Urdhvareta* is the process of forcing the energy into the central channel. When the sexual energy enters the Sushumna, it defies gravity. It rises like mercury in a thermometer.

Hanuman As The Urdhvareta Archetype

Hanuman is often depicted in a specific pose: kneeling, with his mace resting on his shoulder, his hands folded in prayer, and his eyes looking upward. This is not just a pose of humility; it is a pose of *containment*. The mace represents *Prana* (Strength). The folded hands represent *Bhakti* (Devotion). The upward gaze represents *Urdhvareta*.

Hanuman is the only deity in the pantheon who combines absolute physical power with absolute celibacy. Other gods have consorts (Rama has Sita, Shiva has Parvati, Vishnu has Lakshmi). Hanuman stands alone. Why? Because he represents the state where the masculine and feminine energies have merged *inside* the practitioner. He does not need an external consort because his internal circuit is complete.

This completeness is what gives him the power to change his size (*Anima/Mahima Siddhi*). When your energy is not leaking, your density changes. You become heavy enough to crush demons, yet light enough to fly.

The Danger Of Stagnation

A critical warning must be issued here. Many seekers misunderstand Brahmacharya. They think it simply means "stopping sex." So, they stop the physical act. But they do not do the yogic work to move the energy up. The energy is generated, but it has nowhere to go. It hits a dam. Stagnant energy turns toxic. It manifests as:

- Irritability and rage.
- Self-righteousness ("I am holier than you").
- Anxiety and neurotic ticks.
- Obsessive sexual fantasies (the mind doing what the body is denied).

This is why *Urdhvareta* is not passive. You cannot just "not have sex" and expect to become Hanuman. You have to *move* the energy. If you build a dam across a river but do not build a canal to divert the water, the dam will burst. The "Canal" is the breath. The "Pump" is the mind.

The Three Locks (Bandhas)

How do we physically pump the energy up? The Yogis developed a system of pneumatic locks called *Bandhas*. These are muscular contractions that act like valves in the spinal tube.

1. Mula Bandha (The Root Lock): Contraction of the perineum/cervix. This prevents the energy from leaking downward. It seals the basement.
2. Uddiyana Bandha (The Flying Lock): Contraction of the abdomen, pulling the navel toward the spine and up. This creates a vacuum that sucks the energy from the lower belly into the chest.
3. Jalandhara Bandha (The Throat Lock): Dropping the

chin to the chest. This prevents the energy from rushing too quickly into the brain and seals it in the torso for processing.

When these three are applied, the body becomes a pressure cooker. The heat increases. The *Agni* (fire) burns the impurities in the sexual fluid, turning it into gas (vapor/energy), which then rises through the Sushumna.

The Role Of The Tongue (Khechari Mudra)

There is a secret connection between the tongue and the sexuality. In the embryo, the tongue and the genitals develop from the same tissue axis. This is why we often lick our lips when we see something we desire. The tongue is the upper gate; the genitals are the lower gate.

To assist Urdhvareta, the Yogis practice *Khechari Mudra*—curling the tongue back to touch the soft palate (the roof of the mouth). This acts as a "circuit breaker." It connects the front channel (energy going down) with the back channel (energy going up). When the tongue is locked upward, the mind naturally goes silent. The desire to speak and the desire to copulate both diminish. Hanuman is often silent. His tongue is reserved only for chanting "Rama." This is the highest form of Khechari.

The Psychological Shift: From Need To Offering

Urdhvareta is not just mechanics; it is a shift in identity. The "Leaking Vessel" operates from a place of *Need. "I need this pleasure to feel good." "I need this release to feel normal."*

The Urdhvareta practitioner operates from a place of *Offering*. Every urge is viewed as an offering to the higher self. When the wave of lust comes, the Yogi does not fight it. He rides it. He says, *"Thank you for this high-voltage fuel. I will now burn this fuel to light the lamp of wisdom."*

This re-framing is essential. If you fight the urge, you empower it. If you transmute the urge, you empower yourself. You are turning the poison (*Visha*) into the nectar (*Amrita*). This is the path of Shiva. This is the path of Hanuman.

2.4 Sadhana: The Protocol of Conservation

We have discussed the philosophy and the anatomy. Now we must discuss the *How*. How does a modern person—living in a city, working a job, perhaps in a relationship—practice the conservation of energy without becoming a recluse?

This Sadhana is divided into three levels: The Foundation (Diet/Lifestyle), The Practice (Breath/Locks), and The Mindset (Mental Control).

Level 1: The Biological Foundation (Ahara & Vihara)

You cannot transmute energy if your body is toxic. The first step is to clean the fuel.

1. The Sattvic Diet for Ojas Certain foods stimulate passion

(*Rajas*) and irritate the sexual centers. Other foods induce dullness (*Tamas*). For Brahmacharya, we need *Sattva* (purity).

- Eliminate/Reduce: Garlic, onions, excessive chili, alcohol, and heavy meats. These are known as "Rajasic" foods—they increase body heat and make the mind restless, leading to sexual agitation.
- Embrace: Milk, ghee (clarified butter), almonds, dates, honey, rice, and fresh fruits. These are the building blocks of Ojas.
    - *The Hanuman Shake:* A traditional recuperative drink. Blend warm milk (or almond milk), a pinch of saffron, 5 soaked almonds, 2 dates, and a teaspoon of ghee. Drink this before sleep to build the tissues.

2. The Cold Water Protocol (Ishnaan) Hanuman is the son of the Wind, but he is cool in his devotion. Heat in the genitals triggers the urge for release.

- The Practice: Every morning, and ideally before meditation, wash the genitals with cold water. Finish your shower with 30 seconds of cold water on the lower back and perineum. This contracts the capillaries and directs blood flow inward and upward, cooling the *Muladhara* chakra.

3. The Sleep Hygiene Most "leaks" (wet dreams or late-night relapse) happen when the sleep is disturbed or the bladder is full.

- Protocol: Stop drinking water 2 hours before bed. Empty the bladder completely. Sleep on your left side (this activates the *Pingala* or solar nostril, which keeps the metabolic fire active and prevents deep Tamasic stagnation).

Level 2: The Yogic Technology (Kriya)

This is the active transmutation. Do this practice every morning for 40 days to see a shift in your baseline energy.

The "Ashwini Mudra" (The Horse Gesture) The horse (*Ashwa*) is a symbol of vitality. This practice tones the pelvic floor and pulls energy up.

1. Sit in a comfortable posture (Sukhasana) with a straight spine.
2. Inhale deeply and hold the breath.
3. Contract the anal sphincter muscles tight, pulling them upward. Hold for 2 seconds.
4. Release the contraction.
5. Repeat this "squeeze-release" pumping action 10-15 times while holding the single breath.
6. Exhale slowly.
7. Repeat for 3 rounds.

- *Visualization:* With every squeeze, visualize a red light turning into white light and shooting up the spine like a firework.

The "Mahavira Breath" (Transmutation Breath)

1. Inhale slowly through the nose for a count of 4.
2. Hold the breath (Kumbhaka) for a count of 4. Apply *Mula Bandha* (squeeze the root).
3. Exhale slowly for a count of 4.
4. Hold the breath out (Bahya Kumbhaka) for a count of 4. Pull the belly in (*Uddiyana Bandha*).
5. This square breathing with locks forces the energy into the center channel. Do this for 5 minutes.

Level 3: The Mental Fortress (Pratyahara)

The leak starts in the mind before it manifests in the body. You must guard the gates.

1. The 3-Second Rule When you see an attractive person or an image that triggers desire, you have 3 seconds.

- *Second 1:* You notice the beauty. (This is natural/harmless).
- *Second 2:* The mind begins to fantasize or objectify. (The danger zone).
- *Second 3:* You must look away or change the thought. If you linger past 3 seconds, the chemical cascade begins, and it becomes much harder to stop. Train yourself to look, appreciate, and immediately divert.

2. The "Mother/Father" Overlay This is a classic technique from the Bhakti tradition. When Hanuman sees Sita, he sees her as "Mother." When he sees Ravana's queens, he sees them as mothers. If you struggle with lust, overlay the image of the Divine Mother (or a sacred figure) onto the object of desire. It immediately cools the passion and replaces it with reverence.

3. The Transmutation Journal Keep a track of your "Streaks." But do not just count days. Count *Energy*.

- *Entry:* "Today I felt a massive urge at 3 PM. Instead of scrolling, I did 20 pushups and wrote 500 words of my book. I transmuted the energy."
- Celebrating the *use* of the energy reinforces the habit loop.

The 40-Day Mandala

In the Vedic tradition, it takes 40 days (*Mandala*) to break a neurological habit and reset the biological rhythm. I invite you to take the "Hanuman Chalisa Challenge" of the body. For the next 40 days:

1. No conscious release of vital fluid.
2. No pornography or sexually explicit material.
3. Daily practice of Ashwini Mudra (15 reps).
4. Daily consumption of Ojas-building foods.

At the end of 40 days, look in the mirror. Look at your eyes. You will see a shine that wasn't there before. You will feel a density in your voice. You will find that your words carry weight. You are no longer a leaking pot. You are becoming a vessel capable of holding the ocean.

This is the foundation. Now that the vessel is sealed and the energy is rising, we need to learn how to steer it. The steering wheel is the Breath. In the next chapter, we meet Hanuman as *Vayu-Putra*—the Master of the Wind. We will learn how to use the breath to stop the mind.

CHAPTER 3: THE BREATH OF THE FATHER

3.1 The Son of the Wind (Vayu-Putra)

In the pantheon of Vedic deities, lineage is not merely biological; it is functional. A deity's parentage tells us the source of their power and the nature of their operating system. Ganesha is the son of Shiva and Parvati (Spirit and Matter). Kartikeya is the son of Agni (Fire). But Hanuman holds a unique title. He is *Vayu-Putra*—the Son of the Wind.

To the modern mind, "wind" suggests a meteorological phenomenon—the movement of air molecules driven by atmospheric pressure. But in the Sanskrit lexicon, *Vayu* is far more than moving air. *Vayu* is the cosmic principle of movement itself. It is the kinetic energy of the universe. Without Vayu, the sun cannot burn (no oxygen). Without Vayu, the ocean cannot move (no waves). Without Vayu, the mind cannot think (no neural transmission).

Hanuman is the incarnation of this principle. He is the *Dynamic Aspect* of the Divine. If Rama is the Static Self (the Soul), Hanuman is the Breath that animates it. This relationship gives us the master key to the Hanuman Consciousness: To access the Soul (Rama), you must master the Breath (Hanuman).

The Hierarchy Of Control

Why is the breath so central? There is a famous verse in the *Hatha Yoga Pradipika* (2.2) that states: *Chale vate chale chittam, nishchale nishchalam bhavet. "When the breath wanders, the mind wanders. When the breath is still, the mind is still."*

This establishes a hierarchy of control that most modern humans ignore. We try to control the mind *with* the mind. We try to think our way out of overthinking. We try to fight anxiety with logic. This is like trying to smooth the ripples in a pond by hitting them with a stick. You only create more ripples.

The Yogic hierarchy is clear:

1. The Body is ruled by the Senses (*Indriyas*).
2. The Senses are ruled by the Mind (*Manas*).
3. The Mind is ruled by the Breath (*Prana*).

Hanuman represents the top of this hierarchy. He is described as *Manojavam* (swifter than the mind). He is the only one who can catch the mind. If you want to control the "Monkey Mind"—that restless, anxious, chattering aspect of yourself—you cannot do it by willpower alone. You must go to the father of the monkey. You must go to Vayu.

The Mystery Of Mukhya Prana

In the Madhva Sampradaya (a major Vaishnava tradition), Hanuman is worshipped as *Mukhya Prana*—the Chief Life Force. There is a profound story in the Upanishads (the *Chandogya* and *Brihadaranyaka*) called the "Contest of the Faculties."

The senses (Eyes, Ears, Speech) and the Mind argued over who was supreme. To test this, they decided to leave the body one by one for a year. When Speech left, the body became mute but lived. When the Eyes left, the body became blind but lived. When the Mind left, the body became comatose but lived. Finally, *Prana* (the Breath) prepared to leave. As Prana began to uproot itself, all the other senses were violently pulled out, "like a stallion pulling the stakes of his tether." The senses begged Prana to stay, acknowledging its supremacy.

This story illustrates a biological fact: You can survive without sight, hearing, or higher cognitive function. But you cannot survive for more than a few minutes without Vayu. Hanuman, as the son of Vayu, is the *Sutratman*—the "Thread Self." He is the string that holds the pearls of the senses together. If the string breaks, the necklace scatters.

The Two Fathers Of Hanuman

It is important to note that Hanuman technically has *two* spiritual fathers. He is an avatar of Shiva (Consciousness). But he is the son of Vayu (Energy).

This duality helps us understand the goal of our practice. Shiva is the "Zero State"—absolute stillness, the witness, the void. Vayu is the "Infinite Movement"—infinite speed, power, and service. Hanuman is the perfect fusion: Stillness in Motion. He moves at the speed of thought, yet internally, he is as still as the Himalayas.

Most of us are the opposite. Externally, we are sedentary (sitting in chairs), but internally, we are chaotic. The goal of the Hanuman Consciousness is to flip this equation: To be dynamic in the world (Vayu) while remaining grounded in the witness (Shiva). And the bridge between Shiva and Vayu is the Breath.

The Scientific Definition Of Prana

We must clarify what we mean by *Prana*. It is not just oxygen. Oxygen is the physical carrier; Prana is the subtle cargo. In modern physics, we might compare Prana to the electromagnetic field that organizes matter. In neuroscience, Prana is the bioelectric impulse that fires across the synapse.

When we say Hanuman is "full of Prana," we mean he has a high-voltage nervous system. A person with low Prana is lethargic, depressed, and has a weak immune system. Their "battery" is dead. A person with high Prana is charismatic, resilient, and has a magnetic aura. Breathing is the mechanism by which we charge the battery.

Every time you inhale, you are not just taking in air; you are downloading a packet of cosmic intelligence. Every time you exhale, you are uploading your state of being back to the cosmos. Hanuman never forgets this connection. For him, breathing is not an autonomic reflex; it is a sacred communion. It is the constant remembrance of his lineage.

The Kite And The String

Imagine your mind is a kite. It is designed to fly high, to explore, to imagine. But a kite without a string is a victim of the wind. It crashes into trees; it gets lost in the clouds. The breath is the string. If the string is loose (shallow, erratic breathing), the kite crashes (anxiety/depression). If the string is taut and controlled (deep, rhythmic breathing), the kite soars but remains connected to the ground.

Hanuman is the Master of the String. In this chapter, we are going to learn how to hold the string. We are going to learn that the fluctuations of your thoughts (*Vrittis*) are directly linked to the fluctuations of your diaphragm. You cannot calm the kite by yelling at it. You calm the kite by steadying the hand that holds the string.

You are the Son of the Wind. It is time to claim your inheritance.

3.2 The Anxiety-Breath Loop

If you observe the modern human condition, you will notice a pandemic of what I call "Respiratory Failure." We are not dying of asphyxiation, but we are suffering from a chronic, low-grade suffocation. We have forgotten how to breathe.

Watch a person scrolling through their emails or reading a stressful news article. Watch their chest. It is frozen. Or it is moving rapidly and shallowly. This phenomenon has a name: "Email Apnea." We unconsciously hold our breath or breathe shallowly when we are under cognitive load.

This creates a catastrophic feedback loop in the nervous system —the Anxiety-Breath Loop. To break it, we must understand the mechanics of the *Vagus Nerve.*

The Vagus Nerve: The Brake Pedal

The Vagus Nerve is the "Hanuman Nerve" of the body. It is the longest cranial nerve, wandering (hence *Vagus*, vague/wandering) from the brainstem down to the heart, lungs, and gut. It is the primary data highway for the Parasympathetic Nervous System—the "Rest and Digest" mode.

When the Vagus Nerve is stimulated, it acts as a brake pedal. It slows the heart rate, lowers blood pressure, and tells the brain, *"We are safe."* When the Vagus tone is low, the brake line is cut. The body is stuck in Sympathetic overdrive (Fight or Flight).

Here is the critical mechanism: The Vagus Nerve is activated by the EXHALE.

When you inhale, the sympathetic system engages slightly (heart rate speeds up). This is necessary for action. When you exhale, the parasympathetic system engages (heart rate slows down). This is necessary for peace.

The modern "Leaking Vessel" breathes in a panic pattern: Short inhales, short exhales, or breath-holding. This sends a constant signal to the amygdala: *Threat. Threat. Threat.* The brain, receiving this signal, generates anxious thoughts to explain the physical feeling of threat. *"Why am I anxious? Oh, it must be that meeting tomorrow. It must be my finances."* The thoughts then trigger *more* shallow breathing. The loop is closed. The trap is set.

The Monkey Mind (Kapichitta)

In Sanskrit, the restless mind is often called *Markata* or *Kapi* —the Monkey. A monkey does not walk; it jumps. It grabs one branch, then immediately looks for the next. The mind does the same. It grabs a thought about the past, then jumps to a fear about the future. It never rests on the branch of the Present.

Why does the monkey jump? Because the branch is shaking. What is shaking the branch? The Wind (Vayu).

This is the esoteric secret: The mind jumps because the breath is uneven. If you observe your breath during a moment of anger, you will see it is ragged, fast, and heavy. If you observe your breath during a moment of deep focus or "Flow," you will see it is smooth, slow, and silent.

We tend to think that the anger caused the ragged breath. But the Yogis suggest the reverse is also true: The ragged breath sustains the anger. If you can force the breath to become rhythmic, the anger *cannot* sustain itself. The physiological substrate for the emotion is removed.

Hyper-Ventilation vs. Hypo-Ventilation

Most anxiety is actually a form of subtle hyper-ventilation. We breathe too much. We "over-breathe." We think deep breathing means taking in huge gulps of air. But this often flushes out too much carbon dioxide (CO2). Contrary to popular belief, you need CO2. It is the "key" that unlocks the hemoglobin to release oxygen into the tissues (The Bohr Effect). If you breathe too fast (panting), you lose CO2. The oxygen stays trapped in the blood and doesn't get to the brain. The result? Brain fog, panic, and the feeling of "I can't breathe," which makes you breathe even harder.

Hanuman Consciousness is about Hypo-efficiency. It is about breathing *less*, but breathing *better*. It is about "low volume, high efficiency." Think of a marathon runner vs. a panic attack victim. Both are using high energy. But the runner's breath is rhythmic; the victim's breath is chaotic.

The 5.5 Second Secret

Research into heart rate variability (HRV) has found a "resonant frequency" for the human breath. For most people, this magic number is 5.5 seconds in, 5.5 seconds out. That is roughly 5.5 breaths per minute.

When you breathe at this rate, your heart rate and your breath wave synchronize perfectly. This is called Coherence. In this state of Coherence, the "Monkey Mind" stops jumping. It sits down. The intellect (*Buddhi*) comes online.

Hanuman is not just a monkey; he is *Buddhimata Varishtham*—the most intelligent of beings. How can a monkey be the wisest? Because he has mastered the loop. He does not let the wind shake the branch. He *is* the Wind.

Escaping The Loop

So, how do we apply this? The moment you feel anxiety—the tightening of the chest, the racing thoughts—you must stop treating it as a psychological problem. Stop asking *"Why am I anxious?"* Stop analyzing your childhood. Stop trying to "solve" the worry.

Instead, treat it as a physiological glitch. Your kite is spinning. Look at your hand. Look at the string. The string is loose. Tighten the string.

1. Seal the Lips: Mouth breathing is for eating; nose breathing is for living.
2. Extend the Exhale: Make the exhale longer than the inhale. (Inhale 4, Exhale 8).
3. Engage the Diaphragm: Breathe into the belly, not the chest.

By doing this, you manually hack the Vagus Nerve. You force the brake pedal down. Within 90 seconds, the neurochemistry changes. The "Threat" signal stops. The brain looks around, sees no tiger, and calms down.

This is not just "relaxation." This is Self-Mastery. This is the difference between being a victim of your biology and being the master of it. Hanuman does not react to the world; he responds to it. And the space between the stimulus and the response is the Breath.

In the next section, we will go deeper into the breath cycle. We will explore the most potent part of the breath—the part that most people ignore. The Pause. The Gap. The *Kumbhaka*. It is in this gap that the Monkey becomes the God.

3.3 Kumbhaka: The Pause Between Thoughts

We now arrive at the threshold of the deepest mystery in Pranayama: The "Zero Point" of the breath. Most of us perceive breathing as a binary process—inhale and exhale. We see it as a pendulum swinging back and forth. But the Masters know that the power is not in the swing; it is in the pause at the end of the swing.

This pause is called Kumbhaka (Retention). In the ancient texts of *In Search of Zero*, we discussed the concept of *Sandhi*—the gap between two events. The gap between two thoughts is silence. The gap between two moments is eternity. The gap between two breaths is the gateway to the Soul.

When you inhale, you are engaging with the world. You are taking in life. When you exhale, you are releasing the world. You are surrendering. But when you hold the breath—in that precise, suspended moment where you are neither inhaling nor exhaling—you are outside the world. You have stepped out of time.

This is the state of Hanuman in his Great Leap. Visualize Hanuman suspended over the ocean. He has left the Mahendra Mountain (India), but he has not yet touched the shores of Lanka. He is in the void. He is sustained by nothing but his own internal pressure. That suspension is Kumbhaka.

The Physics Of The Pause

Physiologically, why is breath retention so transformative? We are taught to fear holding our breath. We associate it with suffocation. But *Kumbhaka* is not suffocation; it is suspension.

When you hold your breath (especially after an exhale), carbon dioxide (CO_2) levels in the blood begin to rise. As we discussed in the previous section, the modern human has a very low tolerance for CO_2. The moment CO_2 rises slightly, the brain panics and triggers the urge to breathe. This is called "CO_2 Sensitivity." High anxiety is essentially low CO_2 tolerance.

By practicing controlled Kumbhaka, you are training the brain to tolerate higher levels of CO_2. You are raising your "Panic Threshold." This is how Hanuman remains calm in the face of demons. His nervous system is conditioned to withstand the pressure that would make a normal monkey panic. When you can hold your breath comfortably, you can hold your space comfortably. You become less reactive. The world can scream at you, but you remain in the pause.

Stopping Time

The connection between Breath and Time is absolute. In the Vedic cosmology, time (*Kala*) is measured by breath. A human life is not a fixed number of years; it is a fixed number of breaths. When the breath moves, time moves. The mind creates a past and a future. When the breath stops, time stops. The mind collapses into the "Now."

This is why deep meditators naturally experience the suspension of breath. As the mind becomes still, the metabolic need for oxygen drops, and the breath spontaneously pauses. This is called *Kevala Kumbhaka* (The Spontaneous Pause). In this state, you are no longer a biological entity bound by the clock. You are a spiritual entity resting in the timeless *Akasha*.

Hanuman, as the Chiranjeevi (Immortal), lives in this state. He is not subject to the ravages of time because he is not subject to the tyranny of the breath. He has mastered Vayu, so Vayu does not age him.

The Zero Point Of The Mind

Try this experiment right now. Close your eyes. Inhale deeply. Exhale completely. Now, wait. Do not inhale immediately. Just wait in that empty space for 3 seconds.

Notice what happened to your thoughts during those 3 seconds. Did you notice that the stream of mental chatter stopped? It is impossible to think a complex discursive thought while holding the breath out. The "Monkey Mind" needs the movement of breath to swing from branch to branch. When the wind stops, the branch stops shaking, and the monkey freezes.

This is the secret weapon of the Yogi. When you are overwhelmed by a thought loop—worry, anger, obsession—do not fight the thought. Just stop the breath. Apply the brake. The thought will lose its momentum. It will starve for oxygen and dissolve. Kumbhaka is the sword that cuts the knot of Karma in the mind.

The Two Types Of Retention

There are two primary forms of retention we must master:

1. Antara Kumbhaka (Internal Retention): Holding the breath *in* after inhalation.
   - *The Feeling:* Fullness, expansion, power.
   - *The Metaphor:* Hanuman growing to the size of a mountain.
   - *The Function:* It builds *Prana* (Energy) and builds confidence. It fills the chest and heart space. Use this when you feel weak or lethargic.
2. Bahya Kumbhaka (External Retention): Holding the breath *out* after exhalation.
   - *The Feeling:* Emptiness, vacuum, surrender.

- *The Metaphor:* Hanuman becoming small as a cat to enter Lanka.
- *The Function:* It builds *Apana* (Elimination) and destroys ego. It creates a vacuum in the belly (*Uddiyana Bandha*) that pulls energy up the spine. Use this when you feel anxious or arrogant.

Hanuman uses both. He is large when he needs to be (Antara), and he is small when he needs to be (Bahya). He is fluid. He is not trapped in one form because he is not trapped in one breath pattern.

The Danger Of Force

A warning from the *Hatha Yoga Pradipika*: "Just as a lion, elephant, or tiger is tamed gradually, so should the breath be mastered. Otherwise, it will kill the practitioner." Do not force the pause. If you hold your breath until you are shaking and gasping for air, you have failed. You have triggered the sympathetic nervous system and created *more* anxiety.

Kumbhaka must be approached with the gentleness of a lover, not the violence of a soldier. It should be a *caress* of the silence, not a strangulation of the wind. The goal is to extend the comfort zone, not to torture the body. We are looking for the "Sweet Spot"—the moment where the breath is suspended, and the mind is perfectly clear, before the urge to breathe becomes a distraction.

3.4 Sadhana: The Maruti Pranayama

We have explored the lineage of Vayu, the loop of anxiety, and the power of the pause. Now, we must weave these into a coherent daily practice. This sequence is called the Maruti Pranayama. *Maruti* is another name for Hanuman, meaning "Born of the Wind."

This is not a beginner's breathing exercise to just "relax." This is a warrior's protocol designed to build a high-voltage nervous system capable of holding the "Hanuman Consciousness." It consists of three stages: Activation, Balancing, and Expansion.

Time of Practice: Ideally during the *Brahma Muhurta* (4:00 AM - 6:00 AM) or immediately upon waking. Empty stomach is mandatory.

Phase 1: Bhastrika (The Bellows Of Agni)

We begin by generating heat. We must wake up the sleeping energy. Hanuman is often depicted as red-faced. We need to bring blood and oxygen to the brain.

The Technique:

1. Sit in a comfortable upright posture (*Sukhasana* or *Vajrasana*). Spine erect. Shoulders relaxed.
2. Make a loose fist with your hands and place them near your shoulders.
3. Inhale forcefuly through the nose while throwing your hands straight up, opening the palms.
4. Exhale forcefully through the nose while pulling the hands down, closing the fists (as if pulling a chain).
5. Focus on the *sound*. It should sound like a blacksmith's bellows: *Whoosh-Whoosh.*
6. Pacing: Do this rhythmically—one breath per second.
7. Rounds: Do 20 breaths. Then stop. Rest with hands on knees. Feel the "rush" of energy (this is oxygen flooding the frontal cortex).
8. Repeat for 3 rounds of 20.

Contraindication: If you have high blood pressure, heart conditions, or are pregnant, skip the forceful arm movements and breathe gently.

The Subtle Science: Bhastrika clears the stagnant air from the lower lungs. It alkalizes the blood by flushing out CO2 rapidly (temporarily). It acts as a double-espresso for the nervous system without the adrenal crash.

Phase 2: Nadi Shodhana (The Channel Purification)

Now that the energy is awake, we must balance it. We don't want to be manic; we want to be centered. This balances the Left Hemisphere (Ida/Moon) and Right Hemisphere (Pingala/Sun).

The Technique:

1. Use the *Vishnu Mudra* with your right hand: Fold the index and middle finger down. Use the thumb for the right nostril and the ring finger for the left.
2. Close the right nostril with the thumb. Inhale gently through the Left for 4 counts.
3. Close the left nostril with the ring finger. Hold the breath (Kumbhaka) for 2 counts.
4. Open the right nostril. Exhale through the Right for 8 counts.
5. Inhale through the Right for 4 counts.
6. Close the right. Hold for 2 counts.
7. Open the left. Exhale through the Left for 8 counts.
8. This is one cycle.
9. Duration: Perform this for 5 to 10 minutes.

The Key: The exhale must be *twice* as long as the inhale (1:2 ratio). This activates the Vagus Nerve and soothes the "Monkey Mind." Visualize the breath as a thread of light moving up and down the spine, clearing the channels.

Phase 3: The Hanuman Ratio (Samavritti With Kumbhaka)

This is the advanced integration. We introduce the "Box Breath" but with a spiritual focus. We will use the ratio 4-4-4-4.

The Technique:

1. Inhale (Puraka): 4 Seconds. Visualize drawing strength from the earth.
2. Hold In (Antara Kumbhaka): 4 Seconds. Feel the expansion in the chest. Visualize Hanuman growing large.
3. Exhale (Rechaka): 4 Seconds. Release all fear and ego.
4. Hold Out (Bahya Kumbhaka): 4 Seconds. Sit in the Void. Visualize Hanuman becoming small/invisible.

The Progression: Start with 4-4-4-4. As your CO2 tolerance improves over weeks, move to 5-5-5-5, then 6-6-6-6. The goal is not the number; the goal is the *smoothness*. There should be no gasp. The transition between breath and no-breath should be seamless.

Integration: The Breath In Battle

Finally, how do we take this off the mat? You will not always be sitting in a quiet room. You will be in the boardroom, in traffic, in a conflict. This is where the "Hanuman Consciousness" is tested.

When the "Demon" appears (stress/conflict), the Monkey Mind will want to pant. It will want to gasp. You must override the instinct.

The Protocol for Stress:

1. Notice the Gap: Catch yourself gasping or holding breath.
2. The Double Exhale: Take a short inhale through the

nose, and a long, sighing exhale through the mouth. Do this twice. This is the physiological "Reset Button" for the diaphragm.

3. Anchor to the Belly: Place your hand on your navel. Force the breath down. Do not let the shoulders rise.
4. Silent Mantra: Inhale "So" (I am), Exhale "Ham" (That). Or Inhale "Ram", Exhale "Ram".

By controlling the Vayu, you control the situation. The person with the slowest breathing in the room always controls the room. Why? because the person with the slowest breathing has the calmest mind. And the calmest mind perceives reality most accurately.

We have now built the Engine. We have the Body (Chapter 2) sealed and strong. We have the Breath (Chapter 3) deep and controlled. We are no longer a leaking vessel. We are a pressurized vessel ready for launch.

But a rocket needs more than fuel and an engine. It needs a trajectory. It needs a target. In the next chapter, we move to the mind. We move to Chapter 4: The Leap of Faith (Sankalpa). We will learn how to take this gathered energy and direct it toward a single, impossible goal. We will stand on the precipice of Mahendra Parvat and learn how to fly.

CHAPTER 4: THE LEAP OF FAITH

4.1 The Anatomy of a Leap

We now stand at the most cinematic and pivotal moment in the *Sundara Kanda*. The introspection is over. The "Jambavan Effect" has done its work. The silence of the beach has been replaced by the roar of the wind. Hanuman stands on the summit of Mahendra Parvat. Before him lies the Indian Ocean—dark, churning, and impossibly wide. Behind him lies the safety of the land.

This is the universal threshold. Joseph Campbell called it "Crossing the First Threshold." The existentialists called it the "Leap of Faith." In the Hanuman Consciousness, we call it *Langhanam*—The Great Crossing.

It is easy to be spiritual when you are sitting in a cave. It is easy to feel powerful when you are hitting a punching bag. But the true test of power is not how much you possess, but how much you are willing to risk. Potential energy is safe. Kinetic energy is dangerous. To become Hanuman, you must be willing to leave the ground.

The Physics Of The Launch

Let us look closely at the description of the launch in Valmiki's Ramayana. It is not a gentle takeoff. It is violent. The text says that as Hanuman prepared to leap, he crouched down and pressed his feet into the mountain. The pressure was so immense that the mountain began to crumble. Trees were crushed into paste. Water from underground springs gushed out due to the compression. The terrified animals fled. The mountain *sank* under the weight of his resolve.

This gives us the first law of the Leap: To go high, you must first go deep. Isaac Newton defined it as the Third Law of Motion: *For every action, there is an equal and opposite reaction.* If you want to jump ten feet, you must press down with the force of ten feet.

Most people want the flight without the compression. They want to launch a business, write a book, or change their life, but they treat it like a casual hop. They don't crouch. They don't gather. They don't press down into the earth of their current reality. The result is a weak trajectory. They flutter and fall into the water.

Hanuman's compression represents the gathering of all life force (*Prana*) into the *Muladhara* (Root Chakra). It is the moment of absolute tension before the release. You must be willing to "crush the mountain"—to exhaust your current resources, to stress your current limits—if you want to break gravity.

The Void Of Uncertainty

When Hanuman leaves the mountain, there is a terrifying moment. He is no longer on the earth, but he has not yet reached Lanka. He is in the air. He is in the Void.

This is the "Zone of Uncertainty." In business, this is the "Valley of Death"—the period after you have invested your capital but before the revenue starts. In relationships, this is the period after the breakup but before the healing. In spirituality, this is the "Dark Night of the Soul."

The human mind hates this zone. The mind craves solidity. It wants to know where the foot will land before it lifts the other foot. But a Leap, by definition, requires airtime. If you keep one foot on the ground, you are not leaping; you are stepping. Stepping is safe, but stepping cannot cross oceans.

Hanuman enters the sky without a map. He knows the *direction* (South), but he does not know the *destination* (Lanka's exact location). He trusts his velocity more than his visibility. This is a profound shift in operating systems: From Calculation to Momentum. Calculation asks: "What if I fail?" Momentum asks: "How fast can I go?"

The Solitude Of The Flyer

Notice that the army stays behind. Angada, Jambavan, Nala, Nila—they all watch from the shore. They cheer, they pray, they weep. But they do not jump. The Leap is always a solitary act.

You can learn yoga in a class. You can learn business in a school. But the moment of risk—the moment you sign the contract, or speak the truth, or surrender the ego—is a moment of absolute aloneness. This solitude is not loneliness. It is sovereignty. When you are in the air, you have no peers. You have no safety net. You have only your training and your breath.

This terrifies the "Social Self" (the sheep), but it exhilarates the "Spirit Self" (the lion). The Hanuman Consciousness is comfortable with altitude. It does not need the validation of the crowd to sustain its flight. It is sustained by the internal engine of *Bhakti*.

The Flow State (Samadhi In Motion)

Modern psychology talks about the "Flow State"—a zone of peak performance where self-consciousness disappears, time distorts, and action becomes effortless. Steven Kotler and other researchers have identified the triggers of flow: High Consequences, Deep Embodiment, Clear Goals.

Hanuman's leap is the archetypal Flow State.

- High Consequences: If he fails, Sita dies, and Rama's mission fails.
- Deep Embodiment: He is using his full physical capacity.
- Clear Goal: Find Sita.

In this state, Hanuman is not "thinking" about flying. He *is* the flight. The thinker and the doer have merged. This is the state of *Karma Yoga*. When you are totally consumed by the task, when the fear of the future dissolves into the intensity of the present, you are flying. You are in the Akasha.

4.2 Sankalpa: The Vow of Steel

What sustains the flight? Gravity is pulling him down. The demons are rising to stop him. The distance is exhausting. What keeps him in the air? It is not just muscle. It is Sankalpa.

In the West, we translate *Sankalpa* as "intention" or "resolution." But these words are too weak. "Intention" sounds like a wish: *"I intend to lose weight."* "Resolution" sounds like a temporal promise: *"My New Year's resolution."*

Sankalpa is derived from:

- *San* = Connection with the highest truth.
- *Kalpa* = Vow or "that which creates."

A Sankalpa is a Creative Command. It is a statement that aligns the conscious mind, the subconscious mind, and the cosmic will. When a Yogi takes a Sankalpa, the universe is put on notice. It is not a request; it is a restructuring of reality.

The Wish vs. The Vow

Most people live in the realm of *Iccha* (Desire/Wish).

- *"I wish I was successful."*
- *"I hope this works out."*
- *"I'll try my best."*

The language of a wish is passive. It leaves the outcome to external forces. It has a hidden back door: *"If it gets too hard, I can stop."* Because the subconscious hears this back door, it never releases full power. It keeps energy in reserve for the retreat.

Hanuman does not wish. He vows. Before the leap, his internal dialogue is absolute: *"I will search for Sita in the heavens, on the earth, and in the netherworlds. If I do not find her, I will uproot Lanka and bring it to Rama. I will not return without success."*

Notice the absence of "maybe." Notice the absence of "try." This is The Vow of Steel. When you close the back door—when retreat is not an option—the brain switches from "Efficiency Mode" to "Survival Mode." It unlocks resources that are normally inaccessible.

The Architecture Of Sankalpa

How do you construct a Sankalpa? It is not just positive thinking. It has a specific energetic structure.

1. It must be Affirmative (Satya) Do not phrase it in the negative.

- Weak: *"I will not smoke."* (Focus is on smoking).
- Strong: *"I am a clean, healthy vessel."* (Focus is on health).

2. It must be Present Tense (Vartamana) Do not place it in the future. The future never arrives.

- Weak: *"I will be strong."*
- Strong: *"I am Strength."*

3. It must be Single-Pointed (Ekagrata) You cannot have five Sankalpas. You can only have one Major Definite Purpose at a time. Hanuman had only one goal: Sita. He didn't stop to sightsee. He didn't stop to conquer other lands. If you chase two rabbits, you catch neither.

The Seed In The Heart

The ancient texts say that a Sankalpa is a seed (*Bija*) planted in the heart-soil (*Hridayakasha*). For a seed to grow, it needs two things:

1. Protection: You must not dig it up every day to see if it's growing (Doubt). You must not expose it to the harsh heat of skepticism (don't tell everyone your plans).
2. Water: You water it with attention and repetition.

Hanuman watered his Sankalpa with the name of Rama. *Ram-Naam* was the frequency that kept the seed alive across the ocean.

The Practice Of The Vow

In the modern context, we are terrified of commitment. We like to keep our options open. We have "FOMO" (Fear Of Missing Out). But the "Open Option" is the enemy of the Leap. If you keep your options open, you diffuse your Prana.

To practice Hanuman Consciousness, you must take a Micro-Sankalpa. Choose one thing—a project, a discipline, a relationship—and close the exit doors. Tell yourself: *"I am doing this. Even if it hurts, even if I am bored, even if it takes ten years. I am crossing this ocean."*

When you make this shift, you will feel a physical change in the body. The spine straightens. The breath deepens. The anxiety of "decision fatigue" vanishes. You are no longer deciding *if* you will fly. You are simply flying.

In the next section, we will see what happens when the universe tests this Vow. Because the moment you make a Sankalpa, the universe *will* test it. We will meet the Monsters of the Deep.

4.3 Crossing the Void (The Middle Passage)

We have discussed the launch (the start) and the vow (the fuel). Now we must address the most dangerous part of any journey: The Middle.

The beginning is exhilarating. It is filled with adrenaline, hope, and the applause of the crowd on the shore. The end is glorious. It is filled with relief, victory, and the embrace of the goal. But the middle? The middle is silence.

Hanuman is now suspended high above the Indian Ocean. Mahendra Parvat has disappeared behind him. Lanka has not yet appeared on the horizon. He is surrounded by nothing but blue—blue water below, blue sky above. This is the Akasha—the element of Space.

In every great project, in every relationship, in every spiritual practice, there comes a time when the initial enthusiasm evaporates. The "New Year's Resolution" energy is gone. The results have not yet shown up. You are putting in the effort, but the shore is not visible. This is the Middle Passage. And this is where 99% of seekers fail.

The Psychology Of Altitude

Why is the middle so hard? Because the human mind relies on Feedback Loops. When we act, we want to see a reaction. We want validation. We want a signpost that says, "You are on the right track." In the Middle Passage, there are no signposts. There is only the Void.

Hanuman is flying through a feedback vacuum. The only sound is the wind in his ears. The only sensation is the burn in his muscles. The mind begins to whisper: *"Are we there yet?" "Did we miss the turn?" "Maybe Lanka doesn't exist." "Maybe I should turn back."*

This is the test of Faith (*Shraddha*). Faith is not belief. Belief is mental; Faith is visceral. Faith is the ability to hold the vision of the destination when the reality of the present contradicts it. Hanuman sustains his flight not by looking for Lanka with his eyes, but by seeing Lanka in his heart. He navigates by the internal compass of his *Sankalpa*.

The Danger Of Drifting

In the void, the greatest danger is not a monster; it is Drift. When there are no reference points, it is easy to veer off course by one degree. In aviation, the "1 in 60 rule" states that if a pilot flies one degree off course, after 60 miles, they will miss their destination by one mile. Over the distance of an ocean, one degree of drift means missing the continent entirely.

Spiritual drift is subtle. It manifests as:

- "I'll skip my meditation just for today."
- "I'll compromise my values just this once."
- "I'll take a small break."

Hanuman does not drift. His focus is laser-like. He is *Yukta* (yoked) to the purpose. He understands that in the Middle Passage, discipline is not a luxury; it is a lifeline. If he stops flapping his arms (or using his Siddhis) for even a moment, gravity wins.

Vayu-Vega: The Speed Of The Wind

The scriptures describe Hanuman's flight as having *Vayu-Vega*—the speed of the wind. Speed, in this context, is not just velocity; it is Momentum. There is a physics to spiritual growth. It is hard to start (overcoming static friction). But once you are moving, it is easier to keep moving than to stop and restart.

Many of us start and stop. We diet for a week, then binge. We meditate for a month, then quit. This "Stop-Start" cycle destroys momentum. It requires massive energy to relaunch every time. Hanuman maintains a constant, relentless velocity. He does not sprint and rest. He flows.

To cross your own void—whether it is building a business or healing a trauma—you must protect your momentum at all costs. Do not stop. Slow down if you must, but do not stop. The moment you stop in the middle of the ocean, you sink.

The Boredom Of Greatness

We often romanticize the hero's journey as a series of exciting battles. But a long flight is mostly boring. It is repetitive. Stroke after stroke. Breath after breath. Mile after mile of empty ocean.

Hanuman is the master of monotony. He does not need entertainment. He does not need novelty. He finds joy in the repetition because every stroke brings him closer to Rama's service.

The modern mind is addicted to novelty. We swipe, we click, we scroll. We cannot sit in the void. But greatness is born in the void. The writer becomes great not in the moment of publishing, but in the thousands of hours of typing alone. The athlete becomes great not on the podium, but in the 4 AM training sessions where no one is watching.

Hanuman teaches us to embrace the boredom of the middle. To find the "Zero" point within the repetition. To turn the monotony into a mantra.

4.4 Sadhana: One-Pointed Focus (Ekagrata)

We have spoken of the Leap and the Void. Now, how do we train the mind to sustain this flight? The Sanskrit word for this state is Ekagrata—One-Pointedness. *Eka* (One) + *Agra* (Point/Tip).

The mind is naturally multi-pointed (*Vikshipta*). It scatters like light from a bulb. The Yogi trains the mind to become like a laser—coherent, directional, and capable of burning through obstacles. Here are the practices to develop the *Ekagrata* of Hanuman.

Practice 1: Trataka (The Gaze Of The Sun)

Hanuman's first act as a child was to gaze at the sun and leap for it. We replicate this solar focus through *Trataka*—steady gazing. This practice cleanses the tear ducts, strengthens the optic nerves, and, most importantly, freezes the ocular micro-movements that trigger wandering thoughts.

The Protocol:

1. The Object: Light a candle (ghee lamp is best) or use a black dot on a white wall. Place it at eye level, arm's length away.
2. The Gaze: Sit in a meditative posture. Stare at the flame without blinking.
3. The Lock: Let the eyes water. Do not wipe them immediately. The tears carry away the heat (*Pitta*) of the eyes.
4. The Internalization: When the eyes get tired, close them. Visualize the after-image of the flame in the center of your eyebrows (*Bhrumadhya*). Hold it there.
5. Duration: Start with 1 minute. Build to 10 minutes.

The Insight: When the eyes are still, the mind becomes still. When the gaze is fixed, the Will is fixed. This is how Hanuman keeps his eyes on Lanka even when he cannot see it.

Practice 2: The Arrow Technique (Dharana)

This is a visualization to train *Sankalpa* (Resolve). In the *Mahabharata*, Dronacharya asks Arjuna what he sees on the tree. Arjuna replies: "I see the eye of the bird." "Do you see the tree?" "No." "Do you see me?" "No." "Do you see the branch?" "No." "Shoot."

This is Hanuman Consciousness. Total deletion of the peripheral.

The Protocol:

1. Sit comfortably. Close your eyes.
2. Visualize your Goal (Your Lanka) as a glowing target in the distance.
3. Visualize yourself as the Arrow.
4. Visualize your Breath as the Bowstring.
5. Inhale, pulling the string back (gathering tension).
6. Exhale, releasing the arrow (releasing focus).
7. Watch the arrow hit the center of the target.

8. Repeat this 21 times.

This programs the subconscious to ignore distractions. It trains the brain to recognize only two states: *The Archer* and *The Target*. Everything else is noise.

Practice 3: Deep Work Protocols (The Modern Vrat)

To apply this in the modern world, we must create "Sacred Containers" for our work. A *Vrat* is a spiritual vow. We can take a Vrat of Focus.

The Protocol:

1. Eliminate the "Demons": Phone in another room. Notifications off. Internet disconnected (if possible). These are the *Rakshasas* trying to stop your flight.
2. The 90-Minute Flight: Set a timer for 90 minutes.
3. The Vow: "For the next 90 minutes, I am Hanuman. This task is my ocean. I will not touch the ground (distraction) until the timer rings."
4. The Middle Passage: When you hit the 45-minute mark, you will feel the urge to quit. You will feel bored. You will crave a dopamine hit.
5. The Crossing: Recognize this urge as the "Void." Smile at it. Do not succumb. Keep flying.

The Final Insight

The Leap of Faith is not a one-time event. It is a daily practice. Every morning, you wake up on the shore of a new day. The ocean of your duties lies before you. The demons of procrastination and fear are waiting. You have a choice. You can stay on the beach and talk about greatness. Or you can crouch down, press your feet into the earth, gather your Prana, and fly.

You are the arrow. You are the bow. You are the target. *Jaya Hanuman.*

We have successfully launched. We have navigated the silence of the Void. We have locked our gaze on the target. But the ocean is not empty. As Hanuman flies, the waters below begin to churn. Shapes rise from the deep. The universe does not let a Great Soul pass untested. In the next chapter, we meet the three great obstacles that every seeker must face. We enter Chapter 5: Monsters in the Deep.

CHAPTER 5: MONSTERS IN THE DEEP

5.1 Mainaka: The Trap of Comfort

We often imagine that the enemies of greatness are obvious. We expect dragons. We expect demons with bared fangs and swords of fire. We prepare ourselves for conflict, for the "Haters," for the external opposition that tries to crush us.

But in the Hanuman Consciousness, we learn a terrifying truth: The first enemy is not a monster. It is a friend.

As Hanuman flies over the ocean, maintaining his *Vayu-Vega* (speed of the wind), the ocean deity (*Samudra*) decides to help him. He asks the underwater mountain, Mainaka, to rise up and offer Hanuman a place to rest. Mainaka is not a jagged, hostile rock. The scriptures describe it as *Hiranya-nabha*—golden-peaked. It is covered in beautiful forests, sweet fruits, and cool springs. It is a paradise rising from the abyss.

Mainaka speaks to Hanuman with genuine affection: *"O Son of Vayu, you have flown far. You must be tired. Please, land on my golden peaks. Eat my fruits. Drink my water. Rest for a while, and then continue your journey."*

This is the first obstacle. And it is the most dangerous one because it looks like love. It is the obstacle of Comfort.

The Golden Handcuffs

Why is Mainaka dangerous? Because he does not want to stop Hanuman's mission; he just wants to *pause* it. And in the physics of the Leap, a pause is fatal. Remember, Hanuman is flying over water. He is sustained only by his momentum. If he stops to rest, he loses the kinetic energy required to cross the remaining distance.

In your life, Mainaka appears right after your first small success.

- You launch the business, and you make your first $10,000. Mainaka says, *"Good job. Take a vacation. Buy a nice car. Relax."*
- You start a fitness regime and lose 5 kilos. Mainaka says, *"You look great. You can skip the gym today. Have a cheat meal."*
- You begin a spiritual practice and feel a little peace. Mainaka says, *"You are enlightened enough. No need to wake up at 4 AM anymore."*

Mainaka is the Trap of "Good Enough." It is the golden cage of mediocrity. It is the salary that is just high enough to keep you from quitting, but just low enough to kill your dreams. It is the relationship that is comfortable but devoid of growth. It is the seductive whisper that says, *"You have done enough. Why struggle more?"*

The Psychology Of Stagnation

The human nervous system is wired for conservation. It is designed to seek the path of least resistance. Evolutionarily, "Rest" is a reward. But spiritually, Rest is a test.

When you are on a high-stakes mission (finding Sita), "Good Enough" is an insult to the soul. If Hanuman had landed on

Mainaka, history would have ended there. He would have become just another monkey on a golden mountain, eating fruit while Sita waited in agony. The comfort of the present moment is often the enemy of the glory of the future.

This is why high performers often crash not when things are hard, but when things get easy. When the pressure is off, the discipline dissolves. The "Zero State" of awareness is replaced by the dullness of satisfaction. Satisfied people do not burn Lanka. Satisfied people do not find God. Only the hungry find the truth.

Hanuman's Response: The Touch Of Respect

How does Hanuman handle this? This is a masterclass in emotional intelligence. He does not destroy Mainaka. He does not scream, *"Get out of my way, you tempter!"* He understands that Mainaka's intention is benevolent, even if his offer is dangerous.

The scripture says Hanuman simply touched the mountain with his fingertips. He acknowledged the offer. He showed respect. But he did not stop. He said: *"O Mainaka, I am honored by your hospitality. But the work of Rama is not yet done. I have taken a vow not to rest until I see Sita. I cannot stop."*

He touched it, and he kept flying.

This is the strategy for dealing with comfort. You do not have to become a masochist. You do not have to hate comfort. You can acknowledge the "wins." You can touch the success. You can appreciate the nice dinner or the praise. But do not land. Do not let the "Win" enter your head. Touch it, bless it, and use it as a springboard to keep moving.

Sadhana: Breaking The Plateau

Identify your Mainaka. Where have you "landed" in your life?

- Is it your current job title?
- Is it a spiritual plateau where you are just repeating mantras without feeling?
- Is it a creative block where you are relying on old skills instead of learning new ones?

The practice here is Discomfort Seeking. To break the grip of Mainaka, you must artificially introduce friction.

- If your workout is easy, add weight.
- If your work is easy, set a tighter deadline.
- If your meditation is comfortable, sit longer.

Hanuman teaches us that the only true rest is the completion of the mission. Until then, we fly. *Charaiveti, Charaiveti.* (Keep moving, keep moving).

5.2 Surasa: The Test of Competence

Hanuman has passed the test of Comfort. He has refused to settle. Now, the universe raises the stakes. The gods themselves want to test if this monkey is truly capable or just lucky. So, they send Surasa, the Mother of Serpents (*Nagamata*).

She rises from the ocean, a terrifying, shapeshifting entity. She blocks his path and says: *"O Monkey, the gods have granted you to me as food. I am hungry. Enter my mouth."*

This is the second obstacle. Mainaka was a friend offering a carrot. Surasa is a bureaucrat offering a wall. She represents the Obstacle of Ego and Rules. She represents the external world saying, *"You cannot pass. Who do you think you are? You are too small."*

The Contest Of Size (The Ego Trap)

Hanuman, initially, tries to reason with her. He plays the diplomat. *"Mother, I am on a mission for Rama. Let me find Sita first. On my way back, I will enter your mouth."* Surasa refuses. *"No one passes me without entering my mouth. That is the law."*

So, Hanuman tries to overpower her. He expands his body. He grows to 10 *yojanas*. Surasa, being a shapeshifter, opens her mouth to 20 *yojanas*. Hanuman grows to 30. Surasa opens to 40. Hanuman grows to 50. Surasa opens to 60.

This escalation is the Trap of Ego. When we face an obstacle—a difficult boss, a competitor, a legal problem—our instinct is to get "Bigger." We yell louder. We argue harder. We flex our status. We try to out-spend or out-power the problem. But the world (Surasa) is infinite. No matter how big your ego gets, the world can always open its mouth wider. You cannot beat the world at the game of size. If you try to out-ego the world, you will be exhausted.

The Zero Point Turn

Hanuman realizes that this is a losing game. He sees that Surasa is mirroring him. The more he expands, the more the problem expands. So, he does the unexpected. He uses the Logic of Zero.

While Surasa's mouth is gaped open at 100 *yojanas*—a massive, cavernous void waiting to consume a giant—Hanuman suddenly shrinks. He uses his *Anima Siddhi* to become the size of a thumb. In a split second, he darts into her open mouth and flies out of her ear (or comes out instantly before she can close it).

He hovers in the air, tiny and humble, and says: *"Mother, I have entered your mouth. Your condition is fulfilled. The law is satisfied. Now, may I go?"*

Surasa is stunned. She assumes her true form and blesses him: *"Go, O Best of Monkeys. You have passed the test. You possess not just strength, but wisdom (Buddhi). You know when to be a mountain and when to be a mosquito."*

The Art Of Strategic Contraction

This is the deepest lesson of the Surasa episode: Flexibility is stronger than rigidity. In the West, we are taught to be "Big." Be the Alpha. Dominate the room. But the Taoists and the Vedantins know that the hard branch breaks in the storm, while the soft grass bends and survives.

There are times in life when you must be a lion. But there are times when you must be a ghost. When you hit a "Surasa Wall"—a situation that cannot be defeated by force—you must contract.

- Contraction of Ego: Apologize. De-escalate. Let the other person feel they have won, while you quietly achieve your objective.
- Contraction of Needs: If you lose your job, shrink your expenses instantly. Don't fight the reality; adapt to it.
- Contraction of Identity: Be willing to do "small work" to get through a bottleneck.

Hanuman won not because he was strong, but because he was Fluid. He was not attached to his size. He didn't have "Big Monkey Syndrome." He was willing to be small if being small was what the mission required.

Sadhana: The Liquidity Practice

Where are you stuck in a "Size Contest"?

- Are you arguing with a spouse, trying to prove you are "Right" (Big)?
- Are you fighting a market trend that is clearly bigger than you?

The Practice: The next time you face a "Surasa" (an immoveable person or rule), stop expanding. Stop explaining. Stop defending. Drop to Zero. Become totally defenseless. Agree with them. Validate their "mouth." *"You are right. I see your point. How can we solve this?"* Enter the mouth of the problem, understand it from the inside, and slip out the other side.

The Ego wants to be a rock. The Spirit wants to be water. Be water. The rock hits the wall and shatters. The water hits the wall and flows around it.

Hanuman has passed the test of Comfort (Mainaka) and the test of Ego (Surasa). But the ocean is not done with him yet. There is one final monster. And this one does not attack the body; it attacks the shadow. It attacks the very source of his power.

In the next section, we meet Simhika—the Shadow Catcher.

5.3 Simhika: The Shadow Self

We now come to the third and most mysterious obstacle. Hanuman is flying high, confident after outwitting Surasa. Suddenly, he feels a drag. His speed drops. He is flapping his arms, he is applying his will, but he is stuck in mid-air, as if caught in invisible syrup. He looks up. The sky is clear. He looks ahead. The path is open. He looks down.

And there, deep in the waters, is Simhika. Simhika is a demoness with a unique power: She catches the shadow. She does not look at the object in the sky; she looks at its reflection on the water. By clutching the shadow, she paralyzes the substance.

This is a profound metaphor for the Shadow Self (*Chaya*). Mainaka was external (Comfort). Surasa was external (Rules). But Simhika is internal. She represents the unconscious forces—envy, projection, self-sabotage, and past trauma—that drag us down just when we are flying highest.

The Physics Of Projection

Why does the Shadow catch us? In Jungian psychology, the "Shadow" consists of everything we have denied in ourselves. It is the bag of "not-me" that we drag behind us.

- If you deny your anger, it becomes a shadow that catches you in moments of stress.
- If you deny your ambition, it manifests as envy of others' success.

Simhika represents Envy (*Matsarya*). Have you ever noticed that when you are finally succeeding—when you are flying high—you suddenly feel a wave of inexplicable depression? Or you fall ill? Or you pick a fight with a loved one for no reason? You are being dragged by your shadow. You are sabotaging yourself because a part of your unconscious mind believes you don't deserve the flight. The shadow says, *"Come back down to the water. Who gave you permission to fly?"*

The Tall Poppy Syndrome

Simhika also represents the envy of others. When you fly high, you cast a long shadow. People who are stuck in the water (mediocrity) see your shadow. They cannot reach you, so they attack your shadow. They attack your reputation. They gossip. They project their insecurities onto you. *"He thinks he's special." "She's just lucky."*

If you are identified with your shadow (your public image), their grip will paralyze you. You will stop flying to defend your image. You will descend into the water to fight them on their level. And if you enter the water, Simhika wins. She eats you.

The Only Way Out Is Through

How does Hanuman defeat Simhika? He does not bargain with her (as with Mainaka). He does not try to out-smart her (as with Surasa). When he realizes he is being held, he looks down and identifies the source. He sees her open mouth waiting to devour him.

The scripture says Hanuman did something radical. He expanded his body and fell *into* her mouth. He entered the darkness voluntarily. But he did not stay there. He traveled through her throat, tore open her heart (*Marma*), and burst out of her body, destroying her from the inside.

This teaches us the ultimate method of Shadow Work: You cannot run from your shadow. You must enter it. If you feel envy, don't suppress it. Enter it. Ask, *"Why am I envious? What part of me feels small?"* If you feel fear, don't bypass it with positive affirmations. Feel the fear. Locate it in the body. Dive into the mouth of the demon. By fully experiencing the suppressed emotion with the light of awareness (*Sakshi*), you destroy its power. You tear its heart.

Simhika dies only when she is penetrated by the light. The shadow cannot exist when the light enters it.

5.4 Sadhana: The Art of Shape-Shifting

We have traversed the three monsters. We have a map of the resistance. Now, how do we practice this in the laboratory of daily life? The sadhana for Chapter 5 is about developing Psychological Flexibility—the ability to shape-shift like Hanuman to meet the specific nature of the obstacle.

Practice 1: The "Mainaka" Fast (Denying Comfort)

To immunize yourself against the Trap of Comfort, you must periodically reject it. The Protocol: Once a week, practice a "Comfort Fast."

- Sleep on the floor instead of the bed.
- Take a cold shower instead of a hot one.
- Fast from food for 16 hours.
- Drive in silence without music/podcasts.

When you voluntarily choose discomfort, Mainaka loses his power over you. You are training the nervous system to say: *"I appreciate the cushion, but I do not need it."*

Practice 2: The "Surasa" Drop (The Zero-Ego Drill)

To master the Ego Trap, practice "Strategic Incompetence" or "Humble Inquiry." The Protocol: When you are in a conflict or a negotiation and you feel the urge to "Win" or "Expand"—stop. Trigger the "Surasa Drop."

- Physically relax your shoulders.
- Lower your volume.
- Ask a genuine question: *"I might be missing something here. Can you help me understand?"*
- Become the "Thumb-Sized Hanuman."

Watch how quickly the other person's defenses (the open

mouth) collapse. By becoming small, you regain control of the room. You flow through the obstacle instead of crashing into it.

Practice 3: The "Simhika" Scan (Shadow Integration)

To stop self-sabotage, you must catch the shadow before it catches you. The Protocol: Every evening, do a 3-minute "Shadow Scan." Review your day and ask:

1. Where did I overreact? (Anger is often a shadow of fear).
2. Who did I judge harshy? (Judgment is often a shadow of envy).
3. Where did I feel smaller than I am?

When you find a shadow moment, do not judge yourself. Do not say, *"I shouldn't have felt that."* Instead, visualize entering that emotion like Hanuman entering Simhika. Breathe light into it. Say to the emotion: *"I see you. You are a part of me, but you are not the driver."* By acknowledging it, you release its grip on your flight.

The ocean is crossed. The monsters are defeated. Hanuman has navigated the seduction of comfort, the wall of ego, and the grip of the shadow. Ahead of him, the golden towers of Lanka gleam in the twilight. He has arrived.

But arriving is not the end. It is the beginning of the real danger. He is now alone, at night, in the citadel of the enemy. He is a spy in a city of demons. He must find the Light (Sita) hidden in the heart of Darkness (Lanka).

In the next chapter, we enter the Dark Night of the Soul. We enter Chapter 6: The Spy in the Citadel. We will learn the art of resilience, the power of solitude, and how to find allies in the most unlikely places.

CHAPTER 6: THE SPY IN THE CITADEL

6.1 Alone in Lanka (The Psychology of the Outsider)

The sun has set. The roar of the ocean is now behind him. Hanuman stands on the northern shore of Lanka. He has accomplished the impossible—he has crossed the hundred-yojana gulf that separated the despair of the Vanaras from the hope of Sita. He should be celebrating. He should be roaring his triumph to the stars.

But he is silent. He shrinks his massive form down to the size of a normal monkey. He climbs a tree and waits for the moon to rise. He is no longer the celebrated hero leaping from Mahendra Parvat amidst the cheers of his peers. He is now something far more dangerous, and far more lonely. He is a Spy.

This moment marks the transition from the Hero's Journey to the Mystic's Journey. The Hero acts in the daylight, seeking glory and external conquest. The Mystic acts in the dark, seeking Truth and internal alignment. Hanuman has entered the citadel of the enemy, and for the first time in the epic, he is completely, utterly alone.

The City Of Gold And Blood

To understand the magnitude of this moment, we must look at

what lies before him. Lanka is not a primitive jungle outpost. Valmiki describes it as *Suvarna Lanka*—the City of Gold. It is a masterpiece of architecture, wealth, and aesthetic perfection. The streets are paved with jewels; the palaces touch the clouds; the music wafting from the windows is of the highest classical order. It is a civilization at the peak of its material power.

This presents a profound psychological conflict. We expect Evil to look ugly. We expect the demon's lair to be a dark, twisted dungeon. But Ravana's Lanka is beautiful. It is seductive. It represents the pinnacle of *Bhog* (Material Enjoyment). It is the "Corporate Utopia." It is the high-society party. It is the world of glamour, status, and infinite sensory gratification.

Hanuman stands on the periphery of this dazzling city, covered in the salt and dust of his journey. He is a Vanara—a forest dweller. By the standards of Lanka, he is "uncivilized." He does not fit in. This is the archetype of The Outsider.

The Psychology Of The Spy

Every spiritual seeker, at some point, becomes a spy in the world. When you begin to wake up—when you start seeking "Zero" amidst a culture that worships "More"—you realize you no longer fit into the old structures. You go to the same office, but you see the absurdity of the politics. You go to the same parties, but the gossip feels empty. You are *in* the world, but not *of* it.

This is the state of Hanuman in Lanka. He walks through the streets, observing the Rakshasas (demons) drinking, gambling, and boasting. He sees their power, their arrogance, and their deep slumber. They are asleep to the Spirit, drunk on the Ego. Hanuman is the only one awake.

This creates a specific type of loneliness. It is not the loneliness of abandonment; it is the Loneliness of Awareness. When you see what others do not see, you are separated from them by a veil of perception. You cannot share your reality with them because they lack the context to understand it. You become a secret agent of the Divine. You carry the "Code" (Ram-Naam) in your heart, moving through a world that operates on a completely different operating system.

The Discipline Of Waiting

Why does Hanuman wait for nightfall? He has the power to destroy the city single-handedly. He could march to the gates and challenge Ravana. But he chooses stealth. This is a lesson in Prudence (*Viveka*).

There is a difference between Bravery and Bravado. Bravado is the ego screaming, "Look at me!" Bravery is the spirit whispering, "I will do what is necessary." Hanuman understands that the mission is not to prove his strength; the mission is to find Sita. A direct attack would alert Ravana, who might hide or kill Sita. The objective defines the method.

So, he waits. Waiting is the hardest discipline for the "Vayu" temperament. Vayu is movement. Vayu is speed. For a high-energy being like Hanuman to sit still in a tree while the enemy parades below requires immense self-mastery. He enters the Zero State of patience. He slows his breath. He merges with the shadows. He becomes *Nirguna* (without qualities)—invisible, silent, potent.

This "Night Mode" is essential for us. We live in a culture of constant broadcasting. We tweet our thoughts before we finish thinking them. We post our victories before the ink is dry. Hanuman teaches us the power of Secrecy (*Gupta*). Do not reveal your hand. Do not expose your spiritual practice to the ridicule of the cynics. Walk through the marketplace of the world, do your work, pay your bills, but keep your true identity hidden in the cave of the heart. Be a spy.

The Dark Night Of The Soul

In Christian mysticism, St. John of the Cross speaks of the "Dark Night of the Soul"—a period of spiritual desolation where God seems absent. Hanuman's entry into Lanka is the active version of this Dark Night. He is entering a zone where the name of Rama is not chanted. The vibration of the place is *Tamasic* (dark/inert). The atmosphere is thick with lust and violence.

How does one survive in a toxic environment without becoming toxic? This is the question for every person working in a corrupt industry or living in a dysfunctional family. How do I breathe when the air is poisonous?

Hanuman survives by carrying his own atmosphere. He does not inhale the air of Lanka; he lives on the internal breath of Rama. He creates a Micro-Climate of devotion. He looks at the demons and, instead of hating them, he analyzes them. He sees them as victims of their own passions. He maintains the "Witness Consciousness" (*Sakshi Bhava*). He is like a lotus leaf in muddy water—touching it, yet unwetted by it.

The Seduction Of The Shadow

As Hanuman explores the city, he sees things that would tempt any ordinary being. He sees Ravana's harem—women of exquisite beauty, asleep in disarray. He sees varied wines, meats, and treasures. The text says that for a moment, Hanuman felt a flicker of concern. *"I am looking at the wives of another man. Is this a violation of Dharma? Is my celibacy compromised by this sight?"*

This moment of self-doubt is crucial. It makes him real. Even the greatest Yogi must constantly check his compass. But then he applies the logic of the Zero Mind: *"I am looking, but I am not seeing with desire. My mind is not engaged in the enjoyment. To find the Pure (Sita), I must search through the Impure. The gold is hidden in the mud. I must touch the mud to find the gold, but I need not become the mud."*

He realizes that sin is not in the *eye*; sin is in the *intent*. Because his intention is pure service (*Seva*), the visual input cannot corrupt him. He is Teflon. The images slide off.

The Burden Of The Gift

Being the "Spy"—the one who sees—is a burden. When you wake up, you lose the comfort of ignorance. You can no longer enjoy the mindless pleasures of Lanka. You see the cracks in the golden walls. You see the suffering beneath the smiles of the demons. You feel the weight of the mission while everyone else is partying.

Hanuman feels this weight. He is searching house to house, palace to palace, but Sita is nowhere. Despair begins to creep in. *"Have I failed? Did she die? Did Sampati give us the wrong information? Did I cross the ocean for nothing?"*

This is the Valley of Shadows. It is the moment when the Spy feels abandoned by headquarters. But Hanuman does not turn back. He cannot turn back. The ocean is behind him. He digs deeper into his resolve. He moves from house to house, shadow to shadow, driven by a love that refuses to accept the evidence of his eyes.

He teaches us that when you are alone in the citadel, when the night is darkest, when the result is nowhere to be seen—that is not the time to quit. That is the time to switch from looking with your eyes to seeing with your heart. That is the time to become the shadow that hunts the light.

6.2 The Ashta Siddhis (The Science of Situational Power)

To survive in Lanka, Hanuman cannot just be a warrior; he must be a wizard. He cannot rely on brute strength alone, for that would attract an army. He must rely on Siddhis—supernatural powers.

In the *Yoga Sutras of Patanjali*, Chapter 3 (*Vibhuti Pada*) describes the *Ashta Siddhis*—the Eight Great Perfections that a Yogi attains when they master the elements. Hanuman is the master of all eight:

1. Anima: Becoming small (Invisibility).
2. Mahima: Becoming large (Presence).
3. Garima: Becoming heavy (Immovability).
4. Laghima: Becoming light (Levitation/Agility).
5. Prapti: Reaching anywhere (Access).
6. Prakamya: Fulfilling desires (Willpower).
7. Isitva: Lordship (Leadership).
8. Vasitva: Control (Influence).

In the context of the Hanuman Consciousness, we must demystify these. We are not talking about magic tricks. We are talking about High-Level Situational Intelligence. A Siddhi is simply the ability to adapt your energy to the demands of the moment. It is the ultimate flexibility of the ego.

The Encounter With Lankini

The practical application of these powers is seen immediately at the gates of Lanka. The city is guarded not by a soldier, but by a deity—Lankini, the embodiment of the city's prosperity and defense. She blocks the gate. She sees this small monkey trying to sneak in. She roars: *"Who are you? I am the Guardian of Lanka. No one enters without my permission. I will crush you."*

Here, Hanuman faces a choice. He could grow to the size of a mountain (*Mahima*) and fight her. But that would create a shockwave that would wake the city. He could use his mace. But that is a weapon of war, not infiltration.

Instead, he uses a mixture of Laghima (Lightness) and Anima (Smallness) coupled with a precise, controlled strike. The scripture says he hit her with his left fist. In warrior culture, the left hand is the "dismissive" hand. It is used for women (out of chivalry to not use full force) or for unworthy opponents. He didn't want to kill her; he just wanted to reset her operating system.

The blow brings her to her knees. She vomits blood. But in that moment of defeat, she has a realization. The blow wakes her up. She says: *"Decades ago, Brahma told me—'When a monkey brings you to your knees with a single blow, know that the end of the Rakshasa race is near.' You are not a monkey. You are the turning of the Wheel of Time."*

Anima: The Power of Being Underestimated

Let us focus on Anima—the power to become infinitely small. Hanuman enters Lanka the size of a cat (*Marjala*). Why is this a "Superpower"? In a world obsessed with being "Big"—big brand, big voice, big presence—we forget the tactical advantage of being small.

When you are small:

1. You are ignored. The radar of the enemy does not pick you up. You can move through spaces that "Big" people cannot.
2. You gather information. People speak freely in front of the "servant" or the "junior" because they don't consider them a threat. The Spy thrives on being underestimated.
3. You consume less energy. Maintaining a "Big Ego" requires constant fuel (validation). Being "Zero" requires no fuel.

Hanuman's *Anima Siddhi* is the spiritual equivalent of Humility. But this is not the humility of weakness. It is the humility of strategy. He *chooses* to be small so he can win. He condenses his infinite power into a microscopic point to penetrate the armor of Lanka. If he had entered as a Giant, he would have been a target. By entering as a Cat, he became a ghost.

Laghima: The Power Of Levity

Laghima is the power to be weightless. Psychologically, this is the power of Humor and Detachment. Lanka is a heavy place. It is weighed down by the ego of Ravana, the materialism of the demons, and the density of sin. Gravity is strong there. Hanuman retains his *Laghima*. He doesn't let the seriousness of the situation crush his spirit.

Even in the darkest moments, Hanuman has a certain playfulness (*Lila*). He leaps from roof to roof. He observes the absurdity of the demons with a detached curiosity. This "Lightness of Being" is a shield. If you take the toxicity of the world too seriously—if you absorb its gravity—you lose your ability to fly. You get dragged down into depression. The Spy must remain light.

He must float above the drama. He must view the world as a tragic comedy, not just a tragedy.

Garima: The Power Of Unmovable Values

While he is physically light (*Laghima*), he is morally heavy (*Garima*). This is the paradox of the Yogi. Flexible in form, rigid in values. Hanuman changes his shape to fit the situation (cat, giant, brahmin, warrior), but he never changes his core frequency (Ram-Duta).

Many people, when they enter "Lanka" (the corporate world or politics), become shapeshifters in the wrong way. They lose their soul. They become the mask. Hanuman wears the mask, but he never forgets the face underneath. He uses the Siddhis; the Siddhis do not use him. This is Garima—Gravitas. It is the weight of character that commands respect even from the enemy. When Lankini fell, she respected him. Why? Because she felt the *Garima* behind the fist. She felt a moral authority that was heavier than her own.

Prapti And Prakamya: The Physics Of Access And Will

Now we come to the subtler, more dynamic powers that allow the Spy to navigate the labyrinth.

Prapti (The Power of Access): Traditionally, *Prapti* is defined as the ability to reach the moon with one's finger. It implies bridging impossible distances. In the spy's toolkit, Prapti is Resourcefulness. It is the ability to access the inaccessible. How does a monkey enter the most guarded harem in the universe? How does he find the one secret grove (Ashoka Vatika) where Sita is hidden? It is not by luck. It is by *Prapti*. This Siddhi dissolves the barrier between "Here" and "There." It is the mental state where you stop seeing walls and start seeing doors. In the modern world, Prapti is the power of the "Hacker Mindset." It is the ability to bypass bureaucracy, to find the "back door" into the system, to connect with the decision-maker who is supposedly unreachable. When the intention is pure, the universe grants Access.

Prakamya (The Irresistible Will): *Prakamya* is the freedom of will—the ability to move through the earth as if it were water. It represents a state where environmental resistance drops to zero. Hanuman displays this when he moves through Lanka undetected. He is not fighting the environment; he is flowing with it. Psychologically, Prakamya is Flow. When your internal will (*Sankalpa*) is perfectly aligned with the Divine Will, external friction disappears. The guards look away at the right moment. The moonlight falls exactly where you need it. You are in the "pocket" of reality. This is not magic; it is alignment. The world stops resisting the one who has stopped resisting the Truth.

Isitva And Vasitva: The Aura Of Command

Finally, we encounter the powers of Dominion. These are dangerous gifts, for they deal with power over others.

Isitva (Lordship/Sovereignty): *Isitva* comes from *Ishvara* (Lord). It is the power of absolute sovereignty over nature. Even though Hanuman is a "spy" and technically a trespasser in Ravana's kingdom, he never acts like a victim. He walks with the energy of a King. This is Self-Sovereignty. Most people, when in enemy territory, shrink. They become apologetic. They radiate fear. Hanuman radiates *Isitva*. He knows that true Kingship is not about territory; it is about self-mastery. Because he rules his own senses, he naturally rules the environment. This is why, later in the story, when he allows himself to be captured and brought before Ravana, he sits on a coiled tail higher than Ravana's throne. He is the prisoner, yet he is the Lord of the situation.

Vasitva (Control/Influence): *Vasitva* is the power of *Vashikaran* —to bring others under one's influence. It is the power to tame wild beasts and charm enemies. Hanuman uses this subtle influence throughout his stay in Lanka. He influences the mind of Lankini to let him pass. Later, he influences the mind of Vibhishana to turn against his brother. In the corporate or social world, Vasitva is Charisma and Persuasion. It is the ability to change the emotional atmosphere of a room without speaking a word. It is the "Vibe" that makes people want to help you, even when they should be opposing you. But unlike manipulation, which is ego-driven, Vasitva in the Hanuman Consciousness is love-driven. People are drawn to him because he is drawn to Rama. They feel the safety of his aura.

The Siddhis As Soft Skills

In your life, you must cultivate these 8 powers not as magic, but as social agility:

- Anima: Can you be the least important person in the room to learn from others?
- Mahima: Can you expand your energy to lead a team when crisis hits?
- Prapti: Can you find a way to access the resources you need (resourcefulness)?
- Vasitva: Can you influence the emotions of others without manipulating them?

We often think of "Power" as a hammer. But Hanuman teaches us that Power is water. It can be mist (Anima), it can be a tsunami (Mahima), it can be ice (Garima). The form depends on the obstacle. The Spy in the Citadel does not have a fixed personality. He has a fluid toolkit. He becomes whatever the mission demands, yet remains untouched by the transformation.

The Gate Is Open

With Lankini defeated, the gate of Lanka is open. Hanuman steps into the belly of the beast. The moon is high. The music of the demons is loud. The air smells of jasmine and blood. He is looking for one face in a million. He is looking for the Light.

But he will not find her in the palaces. He will not find her in the harems. He will find her in the place he least expects—under a tree, surrounded by monsters, in a grove of sorrow. And before he finds her, he will find something else. He will find an Ally.

In the next section, we will meet Vibhishana. We will explore the mystery of the "Devotee in the Darkness"—how a pure soul can survive in the house of a demon, and how the Spy finds his contact in the enemy territory.

6.3 Vibhishana: Finding Light in Darkness

We have now seen Hanuman as the Warrior, the Leaper, and the Spy. But as he navigates the silent streets of Lanka, searching for the Mother of the Universe, he encounters something that defies his logic. He has entered the city of demons (*Rakshasas*). He expects cruelty, debauchery, and ego. He expects the vibration of "Me and Mine."

But suddenly, amidst the palaces of sin, his ears pick up a sound. It is faint, like a whisper in a hurricane, but unmistakable to ears trained in devotion. *"Ram... Ram... Ram..."*

Hanuman stops. Is he hallucinating? Is this a trap? Why would the name of the Supreme Lord be chanted in the capital of His enemy? He follows the sound. He comes to a mansion that looks different from the others. While Ravana's palace is adorned with weapons and erotic statues, this house is simple. The courtyard is planted not with poisonous nightshades, but with Tulsi (Holy Basil)—the sacred plant of Vishnu. The walls are not painted with blood, but with symbols of the *Chakra* and the *Conch*.

Hanuman is stunned. *"Lanka nisichara nikara nivasa, Iha kahan sajjana kara basa."* (Lanka is the abode of demons. How can a saint live here?)

This is the discovery of Vibhishana. And it represents one of the most profound archetypes in spiritual life: The Devotee in the Darkness.

The Anomaly Of Grace

Vibhishana is the younger brother of Ravana. They share the same blood, the same lineage, and the same power. But while Ravana represents the Inflated Ego, Vibhishana represents the Sattvic Intellect trapped in a Tamasic environment.

This anomaly challenges our binary view of the world. We like to think in terms of "Good Places" and "Bad Places." We think: *"If I go to the Himalayas, I will find God." "If I work on Wall Street, I will lose my soul." "My family is toxic, so I cannot be spiritual."*

Vibhishana destroys this excuse. He lives in the very center of corruption. He eats the food of Lanka. He breathes the air of Lanka. He serves the King of Lanka. Yet, his heart is as pure as the water of the Ganges. He proves that Geography is not destiny. You can be in the middle of a "Hell Realm"—a corrupt corporation, a war zone, a broken relationship—and still maintain a "Micro-Climate" of heaven.

The Tulsi plant in the courtyard is the symbol of this resistance. The Tulsi is delicate. It requires care, water, and sunlight. To keep a Tulsi alive in the scorched earth of Lanka requires immense vigilance. Vibhishana is that vigilance. He is the proof that the environment does not define the individual; the consciousness defines the individual.

The Psychology Of The "Insider-Outsider"

Vibhishana's position is arguably more painful than Hanuman's. Hanuman is an Outsider. He can leave. He has a home elsewhere (Kishkindha). Vibhishana is an Insider. Lanka is his home. Ravana is his brother. He loves his people. Yet, he knows his brother is wrong. He knows the system is doomed.

This creates a state of Cognitive Dissonance and profound isolation. Imagine the whistleblower in a corrupt company who loves the product but hates the management. Imagine the peace-lover born into a violent gang. Imagine the spiritual seeker born into a family of staunch materialists.

Vibhishana cannot speak his truth openly, or he will be killed. He cannot leave, or he will be a deserter. So he lives a double life. He performs his duties as a minister of Ravana during the day, but at night, he retreats to his inner sanctuary and chants "Ram." He is the Spiritual Sleeper Agent. He is waiting. He doesn't know what he is waiting for, but he keeps the lamp burning.

Many of you reading this are Vibhishanas. You feel alone in your circles. You feel that if you spoke your true thoughts—about consciousness, about God, about your values—you would be ridiculed or rejected. So you wear the mask of the Rakshasa (the suit, the social persona) to survive, but underneath, you are wearing the Tulsi beads. Hanuman's arrival is the validation you have been waiting for.

The Meeting Of Two Streams

Hanuman decides to reveal himself. This is a risk. Vibhishana is a demon by birth. He could sound the alarm. But Hanuman trusts the vibration. *Shravanam* (Hearing) has told him the truth. He jumps down from the tree and takes the form of a

Brahmin (a priest). He greets Vibhishana with the code word: *"Jai Shri Ram."*

Vibhishana freezes. He has never heard these words from another set of lips in his entire life. He looks at this stranger. And instantly, the recognition happens. Soul recognizes Soul. The masks fall away. The Demon Prince and the Monkey Warrior embrace.

Vibhishana weeps. He asks a question that reveals the depth of his insecurity: *"O Hanuman, I am a wretch. I am born of a demonic race. My body is made of Tamas. I live in sin. Will the Lord Rama ever accept someone like me? I am not high-born like the sages. I am not pure."*

Hanuman's response is the theology of the Hanuman Consciousness: *"O Vibhishana, look at me. I am a monkey. We are known for being restless, unclean, and chaotic. We are not high-born. If Rama can accept a monkey, surely He can accept a Rakshasa. Rama does not look at birth; He looks at Bhava (feeling). He does not look at the address; He looks at the affection."*

This moment changes Vibhishana's life. It is the end of his isolation. He realizes that he is not crazy. He is not alone. The signal he has been broadcasting into the void for years has finally been received.

The Lotus In The Mud (Pankaj)

This encounter teaches us the principle of Pankaj. *Panka* means mud. *Ja* means born of. The Lotus is born of the mud. Its roots go deep into the filth, into the decomposing matter of the lake bottom. But the flower rises above the water, pristine and untouched. If you drop a bead of water on a lotus leaf, it rolls off.

Vibhishana is the Lotus. Lanka is the Mud. The mud is necessary for the lotus. The resistance of the environment provides the nutrients for the resilience of the soul. If Vibhishana had lived in

Ayodhya (Rama's kingdom), his devotion would have been easy. Everyone chants Ram there. It's the cultural norm. But in Lanka, his devotion is forged in fire. It is muscular. It is chosen, not inherited.

This reframes our struggle with our environment. Do not complain about the mud. The mud is your training ground. The darker the room, the brighter the candle appears. Your presence in a toxic place is not an accident; it is an assignment. You are the Tulsi plant planted there to purify the air.

The Strategic Alliance

From a practical perspective, finding Vibhishana is the turning point of the war. Hanuman is the Spy, but Vibhishana is the Intel. Hanuman knows *how* to fight; Vibhishana knows *who* to fight. He knows Ravana's secrets. He knows the layout of the palace. He knows where Sita is kept (Ashoka Vatika).

This teaches us a crucial lesson in strategy: You cannot dismantle a system from the outside alone. You need an ally on the inside. For every movement of change, there is a need for the "Vibhishana Element"—the insider who has conscience.

- In the corporate world, this is the ethical manager who protects the team from toxic leadership.
- In social justice, this is the privileged individual who uses their access to dismantle the barrier.

Hanuman does not judge Vibhishana for staying in Lanka. He uses him. He understands that Vibhishana's role was to stay behind enemy lines until the moment was right.

The Mirror Of Hope

Before Hanuman leaves, Vibhishana asks for a sign. He needs hope to sustain him until Rama arrives. Hanuman says: *"Wait a little longer. The dawn is coming. The ocean has been crossed. The bridge will be built. Your isolation is temporary, but your connection is eternal."*

This is the message for every "Spy" reading this chapter. You may feel alone in your workplace, your family, or your community. You may feel that your values are alien to your environment. But you are not alone. There are other spies. There are other Hanuman's crossing the ocean to find you. Keep the Tulsi alive. Keep the lamp burning. The rescue party is on the way.

6.4 Sadhana: Night-Time Contemplations

We have explored the solitude of the Spy and the anomaly of Vibhishana. Now, how do we practice this? This Sadhana is designed for the "Dark Night"—for those moments when you feel isolated, misunderstood, or trapped in a hostile environment. It uses the "Zero" methodology to turn loneliness into Solitude and isolation into Sanctuary.

Practice 1: Manas Puja (The Inner Sanctuary)

If you are in a "Lanka" (a place where you cannot openly practice), you must build a temple that no one can see. This is the technique of *Manas Puja*—Mental Worship. It is more powerful than external ritual because it requires higher concentration (*Dharana*).

The Protocol:

1. Retreat: Find a quiet corner. Even a toilet stall or a parked car works. The Spy works with what is available.
2. The Architecture: Close your eyes. In the space of your heart (*Hridayakasha*), visualize a small, lit room.
3. The Altar: Visualize your Ishta-Devata (Rama, Krishna,

Shiva, or simply a Light).

4. The Offering: You have no physical flowers. So, offer your emotions.
   - *Offer your Fear:* Visualize it as a red flower. Place it at the feet of the Light.
   - *Offer your Loneliness:* Visualize it as a blue flower. Place it.
   - *Offer your Confusion:* Visualize it as a grey smoke. Let the Light consume it.
5. The Dialogue: Speak to the Presence. *"I am here in Lanka. It is dark. But You are the fire. Keep me warm."*
6. The Closure: Close the doors of the inner temple. Open your eyes.

The Shift: You have now carried the temple back into the office. You are walking with a secret. The external chaos cannot touch the internal order.

Practice 2: The "Spy" Re-Frame (Cognitive Restructuring)

Most suffering comes from the thought: *"I don't belong here."* We feel like victims of our environment. This practice flips the script. You are not a victim; you are an Agent.

The Protocol: When you enter a toxic environment (a difficult meeting, a chaotic family dinner):

1. The Trigger: As you cross the threshold of the door, touch the frame (like Hanuman touching Mainaka).
2. The Code: Say silently: *"I am entering the Citadel. I am a Spy for the Spirit. My mission is to Observe, not Absorb."*
3. The Mission: Set a micro-goal. *"My mission in this hour is to find one act of kindness (one Vibhishana) or to maintain my breath at 5.5 seconds regardless of the noise."*
4. The Exit: When you leave, shake off the dust. Visualize

the energy of the place sliding off your aura like water off a lotus leaf.

Why this works: It creates Psychological Distance. You are no longer "in" the drama; you are "observing" the drama. This reduces cortisol and protects the ego.

Practice 3: Finding Your Vibhishana (The Ally Scan)

We often assume we are the only conscious people in the room. This is spiritual arrogance. There is almost always a Vibhishana.

The Protocol:

1. Scan the Room: Look at the people around you. Look past their masks.
2. Look for Signs: Look for the quiet ones. Look for the ones who don't laugh at the cruel joke. Look for the ones who look tired of the pretense.
3. The Signal: Send a "ping." Drop a small hint of your true self.
   - *The Verbal Ping:* Mention a book, a concept, or a value that matters to you. "I was reading about stoicism..." or "I value silence..."
4. Wait for the Echo: If they ignore it, they are Rakshasas (for now). If their eyes light up, if they lean in—you have found your Vibhishana.
5. Connect: Build the alliance. You need the support. Even one ally turns a prison into a base of operations.

Practice 4: The 3 Am Protocol (Dealing With Deep Isolation)

There are nights when the loneliness is physical. When you feel the weight of the ocean between you and home. Hanuman felt this.

The Protocol:

1. Do Not Turn on the Light: Stay in the dark. The dark is not empty; it is pregnant with potential.

2. The Earth Touch: Sit on the floor. Touch the ground with both palms.
3. The Mantra of Connection:
   - Inhale: *"I am one with the Earth."*
   - Exhale: *"I am connected to all Seekers."*
4. The Visualization: Visualize a web of light covering the planet. See thousands of other points of light—other spies, other seekers—awake at this very moment.
5. The Transmission: Send a pulse of love to them. *"May you be strong. I am holding the line here. You hold the line there."*

The Insight: You are part of a global grid of consciousness. The separation is an illusion of the ego. In the realm of the Spirit (*Vayu*), there is no distance.

We have survived the night. We have infiltrated the city. We have found the Ally. But the mission is not done. The true object of the search—Sita—is still missing. Hanuman has seen the power of Lanka (Ravana) and the piety of Lanka (Vibhishana). Now he must witness the Pain of Lanka.

He must go to the Ashoka Vatika. He must see the face of Sorrow. And he must learn the most difficult lesson of all: How to give Hope to the Hopeless.

In the next chapter, we enter Chapter 7: The Ring of Remembrance. We will witness the meeting of the Monkey and the Mother. We will learn about the power of grief, the strength of waiting, and the ultimate weapon against despair: The Name.

CHAPTER 7: THE RING OF REMEMBRANCE

7.1 The Garden of Grief (Ashoka Vatika)

Hanuman has navigated the palaces of lust and the chambers of power. He has seen the opulence of Ravana's Lanka—the gold, the wine, the sleep of the unconscious. But he has not found the Mother. The soul is not found in the palace of the ego. The soul is usually found in the quietest, most neglected corner of the kingdom.

Hanuman moves towards a dense grove of trees on the outskirts of the palace complex. This is the Ashoka Vatika. The word *Ashoka* is a compound:

- *A* = No / Without
- *Shoka* = Sorrow It literally means "The Garden of No Sorrow."

This naming is the ultimate irony of the Ramayana. For Ravana, it is a place of pleasure, a botanical masterpiece designed to erase the cares of the world. But for Sita, who is imprisoned there, it is the epicenter of the deepest sorrow in human history. This paradox teaches us a vital lesson: The environment cannot cure the soul. You can be in the "Garden of No Sorrow"—you can be at a 5-star resort, you can have the corner office, you can have the perfect house—but if you are separated from your Source (Rama), you will be in hell. Heaven is not a location; it is a connection.

And Sita is disconnected.

The Face Of Viraha (Separation)

Hanuman climbs a *Simshapa* tree and hides in the branches. Below him, he sees a woman. She does not look like a queen. She is clad in a single, soiled garment. Her hair is matted. She has not bathed. She is thin, emaciated by fasting. She is surrounded by hideous demonesses (*Rakshasis*) who guard her day and night.

But despite the dirt and the despair, Hanuman sees a strange light emanating from her. It is the fire of her chastity (*Pativrata*). It is the heat of her *Tapas*. She is not looking up. She is staring fixedly at the ground, tears streaming continuously.

This is the state of Viraha—Divine Separation. In the Bhakti tradition, this is considered a higher state than union. When you are with the Beloved, you might take Him for granted. But when you are separated, every atom of your being cries out for Him. The mind becomes single-pointed. Sita has no other thought. She does not think of food. She does not think of escape. She thinks only of Rama. She has become Zero. She has emptied herself of all desires, leaving only a vacuum that pulls Rama towards her.

The Inner Critics (The Rakshasis)

Hanuman watches as the demon guards harass her. These Rakshasis are described vividly by Valmiki—some have one eye, some have huge ears, some have no neck. They represent the grotesque nature of negative thoughts.

They whisper to her: *"He is not coming." "He has forgotten you." "You are foolish to wait." "Ravana is a great King. Just accept him and be happy."*

These are the voices of the Inner Critic. When we are in a "Dark

Night," the mind generates these demons. They gaslight us. They tell us that our hope is a delusion. They tell us to "settle" for the material world (Ravana) because the spiritual goal (Rama) is too far away. Sita sits in the middle of this psychological assault, silent and unmoving. She does not argue with them. She simply withdraws into her heart.

The Proposal Of The Ego

Suddenly, the garden goes quiet. Ravana arrives. He comes adorned in all his glory—ten heads representing the ten senses, twenty arms representing his immense agency. He is the ultimate Alpha, the Master of the Universe. He approaches Sita and begs her. *"O Sita, lift your eyes. Look at me. I am the Lord of the Three Worlds. Rama is a forest dweller. He is poor. He is homeless. Why do you waste your youth on a loser? Be my Queen, and the gods will serve you."*

This is the seduction of the Ego. The Ego always tries to impress the Soul with its resume. *"Look what I have achieved. Look at my money. Look at my status."* It tries to convince the Soul that power is better than purity.

Hanuman watches, his blood boiling. He wants to jump down and tear Ravana apart. But he holds his "Zero State." He waits. He watches Sita's response. She does not look at Ravana. She picks up a blade of grass (*Trina*) and places it between herself and the King. She speaks to the grass, not to him. *"O Ravana, you are like this straw to me. Your wealth is straw. Your power is straw. Without Dharma, you are nothing."*

This is the power of Trinavat—treating the material world like a blade of grass. It is the ultimate insult to the Ego. The Ego wants to be hated or loved, but it cannot handle being irrelevant. Sita teaches us that the way to defeat the temptation of the world is not to fight it, but to devalue it. To see it as "Zero" value compared to the Truth.

The Witness In The Tree

Hanuman watches all of this from the Simshapa tree. He is playing the role of the Sakshi—the Witness Consciousness. He sees the suffering. He sees the cruelty. He feels the rage. But he does not act impulsively. If he attacks Ravana now, the mission fails. Sita might be injured in the crossfire.

This is a profound lesson in Titiksha (Spiritual Forbearance). Sometimes, you have to watch the suffering of the world (or your own suffering) without intervening immediately. You have to let the scene play out until the right moment. Hanuman is gathering data. He is assessing Sita's mental state. He realizes that she is at the breaking point. Ravana gives her a deadline: *"Two months. If you do not accept me, I will have you killed for my breakfast."* He leaves. The demonesses return to their torment. Sita is left alone, weeping. She looks at her long hair and thinks of using it to strangle herself. She has lost hope.

This is the moment. The bottom has been hit. The intervention must happen now.

7.2 The Token of Truth (Mudrika)

How do you approach a soul that is on the brink of suicide? If Hanuman jumps down now, a giant monkey appearing out of the dark, Sita will think he is another illusion of Ravana. She will scream. The guards will wake up. The mission will end. He cannot use his form. He must use something else. He uses Sound.

The Melody Of Remembrance

Before he reveals his face, he reveals his frequency. From the branches of the tree, invisible to the eye, Hanuman begins to chant. He does not chant a battle cry. He does not chant his own name. He chants the Ram-Katha—the story of Rama.

"There was a King named Dasharatha... He had a son named Rama... Rama went to the forest to keep his father's word... He killed the demons... He searches for his beloved Sita..."

The sound drifts down like rain on parched earth. Sita freezes. Her tears stop. Who is reciting her secret history in this land of demons? The words act as a Pattern Interrupt. They break the loop of the Inner Critics. For months, she has only heard abuse. Now, she hears the Truth. The sound prepares her heart to receive the vision. This confirms the Vedic principle: *Shravanam* (Hearing) must precede *Darshanam* (Seeing).

The Drop

Hanuman sees that she is alert. He pauses. Then, with infinite delicacy, he drops an object from the tree. It falls through the leaves and lands in her lap. It is a ring. The Anguliya. The Ring of Rama. It is engraved with the name *"Rama"* in gems.

Sita stares at it. Valmiki writes that she looked at the ring as if she were looking at Rama's soul. She touched it to her eyes. She pressed it to her heart. For a moment, the Ashoka Vatika vanished. The demons vanished. She was back in Ayodhya. She was with Him.

The Psychology Of The Token

Why is the Ring so powerful? It is a Token of Remembrance. In the "Search for Zero," we often talk about the formless. But the human mind cannot hold the formless for long, especially in times of crisis. We need a form. We need an anchor.

The Ring represents the Tangible Proof of Connection. When you are in the "Lanka" of depression or failure, the mind argues that God has abandoned you. It argues that your spiritual past was a hallucination. You need a "Ring"—a specific memory, a specific book, a specific mantra, or a physical object—that proves the connection is real.

- For a soldier, it might be a photo of his family.
- For a seeker, it might be the *Mala* given by the Guru.
- For the addict in recovery, it is the sobriety chip.

The Ring is the bridge between the memory of the light and the reality of the dark. It tells Sita: *"You are not crazy. He exists. He remembers you."* The ring breaks the spell of isolation.

The Reveal: Establishing Trust

Sita looks up. She sees the monkey. Her first reaction is fear. *"Is this Ravana in disguise?"* Hanuman jumps down. He is small, humble, hands folded in *Anjali Mudra*. He does not start with, "I am the great Hanuman." He starts with, "I am the servant of Rama." (*Rama Duta*).

Sita interrogates him. She is wise. She tests him. *"Describe Rama to me. If you are truly his messenger, tell me his signs."* Hanuman describes Rama's body, his voice, his walk, and his character with such intimacy and detail that Sita breaks down. Only someone who loved Rama could describe Him like that. Trust is established.

The Shift: From Victim To Warrior

This moment marks the turning point of the entire epic. Before the Ring, Sita was a victim waiting to die. After the Ring, she is a warrior waiting to be rescued. Hope has returned. And hope is a biological force. It reignites the will to live.

Hanuman offers to carry her back on his back immediately. *"Mother, climb on my back. I will cross the ocean and take you to Rama right now."* This is the Impulse of the Hero. He wants to fix it *now*.

But Sita refuses. And her refusal is profound. She says: *"No, Hanuman. If you steal me back, it is essentially the same as Ravana stealing me. It is theft. Rama must come. He must defeat the darkness openly. He must redeem my honor and his own. It is not enough to be saved; I must be vindicated."*

She chooses the harder path. She chooses to wait longer so that the victory can be complete. She gives Hanuman a token in return—the *Chudamani* (Jewel from her hair). The circuit is complete. The message has been delivered. The response has been received.

Sadhana: Creating Your Ring

We cannot wait for a monkey to drop a ring from a tree. We must carry our own rings. This Sadhana is about creating an Anchor of Hope.

The Protocol:

1. Identify Your Anchor: Choose a physical object that represents your highest self or your deepest connection to the Divine. It could be a ring, a necklace, a stone, or a small photo.
2. Charge the Anchor: Hold it in your hand during your deepest meditation. Pour your "Zero State" into it. Chant your mantra into it. Make it radioactive with your intention.
3. The Deployment: Wear it or carry it daily. But here is the key—when you are in a "Lanka" moment (stress, conflict, despair), touch it.
4. The Recall: Let the physical sensation of the object instantly trigger the memory of who you are.

- *"I am not this stress. I am the one who wears the Ring."*
- *"I am not this failure. I am the servant of the Light."*

Use the object to snap out of the hypnotic trance of the world. The Ring is your reality check.

Hanuman has found Sita. He has delivered the hope. The mission is technically 90% complete. A prudent spy would leave now. He should sneak out, cross the ocean, and report back. But Hanuman is not just a spy. He is *Vayu-Putra*. He looks at the beautiful grove of Ashoka Vatika. He looks at the arrogance of Ravana's guards. He thinks: *"The mission is done. But the lesson is not yet taught."*

He decides to go off-script. He decides to start a war. In the next chapter, we see the shift from Stealth to Rage. We enter Chapter 8: Controlled Chaos. We will see Hanuman smash the garden, slaughter the armies, and finally, burn the city of gold. We will learn the difference between destruction and purification.

CHAPTER 8: CONTROLLED CHAOS

8.1 The Dignity of Anger (Dharma-Krodha)

We have arrived at the moment where the silence of the Spy must be shattered by the roar of the Lion. Hanuman has successfully infiltrated the citadel. He has located the Soul (Sita) in the Ashoka Vatika. He has delivered the Token of Remembrance (The Ring). He has restored hope where there was only despair. From a strategic perspective, the mission is complete. The "Objective Key Result" (OKR) was to find Sita and report back. The prudent path—the path of the efficient bureaucrat or the careful spy—would be to slip back into the shadows, swim across the ocean, and deliver the intelligence to Rama. It is the safe choice. It is the logical choice.

But Hanuman does not move. He sits perched on the high wall of the *Ashoka Vatika*, looking down at the manicured perfection of Ravana's garden. He observes the lush trees, the crystal fountains, the golden pathways, and the demonic guards who have spent months tormenting the Mother of the Universe. He looks at the opulence of a civilization built entirely on the foundation of stolen Dharma. And in the center of his chest, something begins to rise. It is not peace (*Shanti*). It is not the cool, detachment of the witness (*Sakshi*). It is heat. It is fire. It is Krodha (Anger).

But we must be very precise here. This is not the petty anger of a wounded ego. This is not the tantrum of a child denied a toy, nor the road rage of a commuter stuck in traffic. This is something far more ancient and far more terrifying. This is the roaring, volcanic indignation of the Cosmos witnessing injustice. This is Dharma-Krodha—Righteous Anger.

Hanuman decides, in this moment, to go off-script. He decides that it is not enough to merely *find* the Truth; one must also *expose* the Lie. He realizes that leaving Lanka untouched would be a form of complicity. To leave the machinery of oppression intact is to permit it to continue grinding. So, he stands up. He breathes into his solar plexus. He expands his form. And he begins to smash the garden.

The Myth Of The Passive Yogi

We must pause on this wall with Hanuman to dismantle one of the most dangerous misconceptions in modern spirituality: The Myth of the Passive Yogi. We have been sold a sanitized, domesticated version of spirituality. We imagine the "Enlightened Being" as a perpetual doormat—someone who smiles softy at abuse, accepts corruption with a polite "Namaste," and bypasses all conflict in the name of "good vibes" or "high vibration." We have confused Ahimsa (Non-Violence) with Impotence.

But let us look at the archetype of Hanuman. He is *Yogi-Raj*—the King of Yogis. He is the master of the mind, the conqueror of the senses (*Jitendriya*). He possesses the perfect stillness of the Himalayas. And yet, look at him now. He is tearing up thousand-year-old trees by their roots. He is smashing the marble pavilions into dust. He is turning the pleasure ponds into mud. He is dismantling the aesthetic beauty of the ego with brutal efficiency.

Why? Because true spirituality is not the *absence* of power; it is the *control* of power. To be harmless is not a virtue if it comes from helplessness. A rabbit is harmless because it *cannot* kill. A lion is harmless only when it *chooses* not to kill. Hanuman is the Lion. He teaches us that there is a time for silence, and there is a time for the roar. There is a time to sit in the cave, and there is a time to burn the city. The spiritual person who cannot access their aggression is not spiritual; they are merely repressed. They are not peaceful; they are paralyzed. Hanuman destroys the garden to send a clear, unequivocal signal to Ravana: *"Do not mistake our silence for weakness. Do not mistake our patience for cowardice. We are coming."*

The Psychology Of Provocation

Hanuman's destruction of the Ashoka Vatika is not a random act of vandalism. It is a calculated military strategy known as Provocation. Hanuman is a Spy, but he is also a General. He needs intel that he cannot get from the shadows. He wants to draw the enemy out. He wants to stress-test the system. By creating chaos, he forces the hidden structure of Lanka to reveal itself. He wants to know:

- How fast do they mobilize?
- Who are their commanders?
- What is the hierarchy of their response?
- Do they fight with discipline, or do they fight with rage?

Chaos is information. In your own life, you will often find yourself in "Lanka"—a toxic workplace, a stagnant relationship, or a corrupt system. The system maintains itself through a veneer of "civilized" silence. Everyone knows the boss is corrupt, but no one speaks. Everyone knows the family dynamic is abusive, but everyone smiles at dinner. In such situations, maintaining the "peace" only serves to uphold the dysfunction. Sometimes, you have to break the furniture. You have to speak the uncomfortable truth. You have to disrupt the flow of "business as usual." You have to stop covering for the incompetence of others. When you disrupt the system, the masks fall off. You see who people really are. You see who runs for cover, who attacks, and who stands with you. Hanuman breaks the garden to strip Ravana of his illusion of control.

The Hierarchy Of Force

The response from Lanka is swift, and it allows us to witness the Hierarchy of Force. Hanuman does not use the same level of violence for every opponent. He scales his aggression with surgical precision.

First, Ravana sends the Kinkaras—eighty thousand servant warriors. These represent the "nuisances" of life—the petty bureaucrats, the trolls, the minor obstacles. Hanuman does not even use a weapon against them. He does not waste his *Prana*. He simply rips up an iron bar from the gate and spins it. He uses the environment against them. He treats them with the disdain they deserve. *Lesson:* Do not use a cannon to kill a mosquito. Preserve your energy.

Next, Ravana sends Jambumali, the son of the commander Prahasta. He is a skilled archer. He represents a legitimate threat—a competitor, a skilled rival. Hanuman engages him. He catches a rock thrown by the demon, spins it, and hurls it back. He meets skill with superior skill. He smashes him.

Then, Ravana sends the Seven Sons of Ministers. These represent the "Establishment"—the people who have power only because of their position, not their merit. Hanuman turns them to dust.

Finally, Ravana sends his own son, Aksha Kumara. Aksha is a brilliant young warrior. He is skilled, brave, and noble in his own way. He wounds Hanuman. The scripture says that for a moment, Hanuman paused and admired the boy's dexterity. He felt a pang of regret that such talent was wasted on the side of Adharma. But Hanuman applies the Zero Mind. He realizes that compassion here would be cruelty to the larger mission. If he spares the boy, the boy will kill others. He flies up, grabs Aksha by his legs, spins him like a wheel of fire, and throws him to the ground. The Prince is dead.

This escalation teaches us that the spiritual warrior is not a sadist. He does not enjoy the killing. But he does not flinch from it. He uses the minimum force necessary to stop the evil, but *no less* than necessary. He is a surgeon. The surgeon cuts flesh, spills blood, and causes pain. But the surgeon is not a murderer. The intent is healing. Hanuman is performing surgery on Lanka. He is cutting out the tumor of arrogance, layer by layer.

The Flow State Of Aggression

Notice the geometry of Hanuman's violence. Most of us, when we get angry, become rigid. Our shoulders rise, our breath stops (the "Email Apnea" we discussed earlier), our vision tunnels, and our IQ drops. We become stupid in our rage. We flail. Hanuman gets angry, but he stays loose. He is constantly moving, leaping, changing size (*Anima* to *Mahima*). He uses the pillar of the palace as a mace. He uses the bodies of the demons as projectiles. This is Flow State Aggression. It is violence without tension.

He is breathing rhythmically. His mind (*Buddhi*) is sharp, calculating vectors and velocities even as he crushes skulls. This is Controlled Chaos. It is the ability to hold the center of the cyclone. You can be in the middle of a shouting match, a high-stakes lawsuit, or a physical crisis, and yet, the center of you is watching, calculating, and breathing 5.5 seconds in, 5.5 seconds out. The "Zero" is present even in the heat of battle. This is the state we aim for. Not the absence of conflict, but the mastery of it. We aim to be dangerous, but disciplined.

8.2 The Tail on Fire (The Burning of Ego)

The death of Aksha Kumara shakes Ravana to his core. He realizes this is no ordinary monkey. The "pest" has become a "calamity." He sends his greatest warrior, his eldest son, Indrajit (The

Conqueror of Indra). Indrajit is a master of sorcery (*Maya*) and celestial weapons. He fights from the clouds, invisible. He realizes he cannot defeat Hanuman physically—the monkey is too fast, too strong. So, Indrajit uses the nuclear option. He invokes the Brahmastra—the weapon of Creator Brahma.

When the weapon is fired, Hanuman recognizes it immediately. He knows he has a boon from Brahma that makes him immune to it for the most part. He could easily shrug it off or dodge it. But Hanuman is not just a warrior; he is a devotee. He knows the protocol. *You must bow to the Brahmastra.* If he resists it, he insults the Creator. He insults the very source of his own power. So, Hanuman makes a strategic choice that baffles the demons: He Surrenders. He allows the weapon to bind him. He falls to the ground, paralyzed.

The demons rush in. They cheer. They mock him. And in their ignorance, they tie him up with ordinary jute ropes. (Note the profound irony here: The scriptures say that the moment the demons bound him with physical ropes, the power of the celestial Brahmastra faded, because the Divine Weapon cannot coexist with the bondage of earthly material. But Hanuman stays bound voluntarily. Why? Because he has been waiting for an invitation to the Throne Room. He wants to meet the King.)

The Audience With The Ego

Hanuman is dragged into the court of Ravana. It is a spectacle of intimidation. Ravana sits on a high crystal throne, radiating dark, majestic power. The court is filled with ministers, generals, and spies. They look down at the bound monkey with contempt. Hanuman stands before him, unbowed. They give him no seat. This is a diplomatic insult. So, Hanuman creates his own seat. He lengthens his tail (*Mahima Siddhi*). He coils it round and round, higher and higher, until it forms a pillar that towers above Ravana's throne. He climbs up, sits on the top of his tail, and looks down at the ten-headed King.

This is Isitva (The Siddhi of Lordship) in action. He is sending a non-verbal message: *"You may have captured my body, but you cannot capture my status. I am the servant of Rama, and therefore I am higher than you. My seat is not given by you; it is created by me."*

The dialogue that follows is one of the greatest debates in Vedantic history. Ravana asks: *"Who are you? Who sent you? Why did you destroy my garden?"* Hanuman replies with absolute clarity, devoid of fear: *"I am the messenger of Rama. I destroyed the garden because I was hungry. I killed your soldiers because they attacked me. Self-defense is the law of nature. O Ravana, listen to me. You are a great scholar. You have performed immense Tapasya. You are a devotee of Shiva. Why do you destroy all this merit for the sake of one woman? Sita is not a woman; she is the Night of Death for you. She is the coiled serpent of your doom. Return her. Make peace. Rama is the ocean of mercy. He will forgive you. Do not let your ego destroy your race."*

Hanuman speaks Truth to Power. He gives the Ego one last chance to repent. He offers a lifeline. But the Ego, blinded by pride, cannot hear. The Ego interprets correction as an insult. Ravana, furious, orders Hanuman's death.

The Humiliation Ritual

Vibhishana, the voice of reason, intervenes. *"You cannot kill a messenger (Duta). It is against the laws of war (Rajneeti). If you kill him, who will take the message to Rama? Who will bring Rama here so you can fight him?"* Ravana agrees, but his sadism seeks a loophole. *"Fine. I won't kill him. But a monkey is proud of his tail. It is his ornament. Set his tail on fire. Let him go back to his master maimed, scarred, and humiliated. Let him be a warning."*

The demons laugh. They wrap Hanuman's tail in old, oily rags. They pour ghee and oil. They set it ablaze. They parade him through the streets of Lanka. *"Look at the thief! Look at the monkey with the burning tail!"* They drum, they jeer, they spit on him. The women laugh from the balconies. The children throw stones.

This is the ultimate Humiliation Ritual. In your life, this is the moment when you are publicly shamed. When you are fired and escorted out of the building. When your reputation is attacked on social media. When you are the laughingstock of your community. It is the fire that is meant to burn your self-worth. It is the world saying, *"You are nothing."*

The Cool Fire (The Alchemy Of Grace)

But something strange is happening. News reaches Sita in the garden that Hanuman is being burned. She closes her eyes. She enters the fire of her own chastity. She prays to Agni (The Fire God): *"If I have been faithful to Rama, if I have any merit, O Fire, be cool to Hanuman. Do not burn him."*

Hanuman feels the fire on his tail, but he feels no pain. He says: *"It feels like sandalwood paste. It feels like ice. The fire is dancing, but it does not bite."* This is the Alchemy of Grace. When you are walking the path of Truth, the fire of the world cannot burn you. The insults of the ignorant turn into blessings. The humiliation becomes a coronation. Hanuman realizes the cosmic joke. *"They think they are punishing me. They think they are shaming me. But they have just handed me a torch. They have given me the very weapon I need to complete my mission."*

The Transmutation Of Pain

This is the pivot point of the chapter. Hanuman breaks the ropes (which he could have done anytime). He leaps into the sky. His tail is a blazing comet, streaking across the night sky of Lanka. He looks at the golden city below—the city of arrogance, the city that imprisons the Mother. And he decides to clean it.

This is Transmutation. Hanuman took the very thing Ravana used to hurt him (the fire) and used it to destroy Ravana's power. This is the ultimate "Zero" move. "You gave me pain? Thank you. I will use this pain as fuel." "You gave me humiliation? Thank you. I will use it to burn down your ego." "You gave me a crisis? Thank you. I will use it to transform."

Never waste a crisis. Never waste an insult. When the world sets your tail on fire, do not cry. Do not play the victim. Use the light to see clearly, and use the heat to burn the rubbish in your life.

8.3 Constructive Destruction

We now come to the most radical aspect of the Hanuman Consciousness: The willingness to destroy. In most civilized societies, destruction is viewed as "bad." We value preservation. We value "keeping the peace." We hoard old structures, old memories, and old systems because we are afraid of the void that follows collapse. But Hanuman is an incarnation of Shiva—the Destroyer. His burning of Lanka is not a tragedy; it is a Purification. Fire (*Agni*) is the only element that does not get polluted. If you throw filth into water, the water gets dirty. If you throw filth into fire, the filth turns to ash, and the fire remains fire. Hanuman's fire is the fire of Truth. It burns everything that is false.

The False Structure

Why did Lanka need to burn? Because it was built on a lie. It was a golden city, yes. It was prosperous, yes. But its foundation was *Adharma* (unrighteousness). It was sustained by the suffering of the sages and the kidnapping of Sita. It was a monument to the Ego. Such a structure cannot be "reformed." You cannot renovate a house built on a sinkhole. You cannot "fix" a relationship that is abusive at its core. You cannot "tweak" a career that violates your soul. You must raze it to the ground and start over.

In your life, you are often living in a personal Lanka.

- It might be a career built on impressing others rather than your own passion.
- It might be a relationship that drains your soul but provides financial security (Gold).
- It might be a habit loop of addiction that gives you temporary pleasure (Bhog). You try to "fix" it. You paint the walls. You rearrange the furniture. You try to be "positive." But Hanuman says: "Burn it." Stop maintaining the structure of your own misery. If the foundation is rotten, the only spiritual act is destruction.

The Fear Of Ash (Bhasma)

Why do we hesitate to burn our Lankas? Because we are terrified of the Ash. We are terrified of who we will be without our titles, our security, and our familiar pains. We prefer a "Golden Prison" to a "Free Void." But Hanuman teaches us that Ash (*Bhasma*) is sacred. In the Shiva tradition, ash represents the ultimate reality —that which remains when everything impermanent is gone. When Hanuman burns Lanka, he is stripping Ravana of his illusions. He is showing Ravana: *"Look, your gold melts. Your palaces fall. Your weapons turn to smoke. What is left? Only the Soul. Save that."*

When you burn a toxic relationship or quit a soul-sucking job, you enter the Ash phase. It feels empty. It feels scary. But in that emptiness, the new (Rama) can finally enter. You cannot invite Rama into a house that is full of Ravana's furniture. You must clear the space. You must create the vacuum.

Surgical Destruction (The Vibhishana Exception)

However, notice the precision of Hanuman's fire. He jumps from roof to roof. He burns the armory. He burns the stables. He burns the treasury. He burns the palaces of the generals. But he spares the house of Vibhishana. And he spares the Ashoka Vatika where Sita lives.

This is Constructive Destruction. It is surgical. It is discriminatory (*Viveka*). Many people, when they start their spiritual journey, become "Reckless Destroyers." They read a book on detachment and quit their jobs without a plan. They dump their supportive families. They burn bridges out of ego-driven rage or manic impulse. This is not Hanuman Consciousness; this is a tantrum. This is foolishness.

Hanuman protects the seed of the good (Vibhishana) while destroying the structure of the bad (Ravana). Before you burn your life down, you must ask: *"Where is the Vibhishana in this situation?" "What is valuable here that I must protect?"*

- Destroy the bad habit, but keep the discipline it taught you.
- End the relationship, but preserve the capacity to love.
- Quit the job, but keep the skills and the network.

True destruction burns the chaff and saves the wheat. It is an act of love, not hate.

8.4 Sadhana: The Warrior's Meditation

How do we practice "Controlled Chaos" in our daily lives? Most meditation techniques are designed to calm you down. They are "Water" practices. They are about acceptance and flow. But sometimes, you need a "Fire" practice. You need to access the Warrior Energy to break through lethargy (*Tamas*) or fear. You need to release the trapped aggression in a safe, sacred container.

This Sadhana is derived from the martial traditions of *Kalaripayattu* (the ancient Indian martial art) and the tantric practice of *Agni-Sara*.

Practice 1: The Woodchopper (Kashtha-Chedana)

This is a dynamic somatic release technique. It uses sound and motion to release trapped rage from the solar plexus (*Manipura Chakra*). Anger is often stored in the belly and the jaw. This practice unlocks both.

The Protocol:

1. Stance: Stand with feet shoulder-width apart, knees slightly bent (Horse Stance). Feel rooted in the earth.
2. Grip: Interlace your fingers and extend your arms downwards. Imagine you are holding a heavy, sharp axe.
3. The Wind-Up: Inhale deeply through the nose while raising your arms straight over your head. Arch your back slightly. Look up.
   - *Visualization:* Visualize the "Lanka" (the obstacle, the addiction, the fear) sitting on a wood block between your feet.
4. The Strike: Exhale forcefully and explosively through the mouth with the sound "HA!" while swinging the axe down between your legs.
   - *Note:* Do not hit the floor; stop the motion with control just above the ground. This "braking" action engages the core.
5. The Release: Let the upper body hang loose for a second.
6. Repetition: Do this 21 times continuously.
7. The Outcome: You will feel a rush of heat and a lightness in the chest. The "HA" sound acts as a sonic purgative, expelling stale air and pent-up emotion.

Practice 2: The Sword In The Sheath (Visualiza-

tion)

This practice is for integrating aggression so that you are dangerous but disciplined. It trains the nervous system to hold high-voltage energy without acting it out destructively.

The Protocol:

1. Sit: In a comfortable meditative posture. Spine erect. Eyes closed.
2. Visualize: Imagine a sword of pure white light floating in your spinal column. The tip of the sword is at the base of the spine (*Muladhara*); the handle is at the base of the skull (*Medulla*).
3. The Sheath: Now, visualize a golden sheath covering this sword. The sheath represents your *Viveka* (Wisdom) and *Control.*
4. The Breath:
   - Inhale: Visualize drawing the sword slightly out of the sheath (about an inch). Feel the raw power, the sharpness, the potential for destruction. Feel the adrenaline spike slightly.
   - Exhale: Slide the sword back into the sheath with a distinct "click." Feel the peace of contained power. Feel the relaxation.
5. The Mantra: With each cycle, silently affirm: *"I am the Master of my Fire. I am dangerous, therefore I am peaceful."*

The Insight: A harmless man is not peaceful; he is just harmless. A dangerous man who keeps his sword sheathed is the definition of a Yogi.

Practice 3: The Burn List (Likhita Agni)

Use this when you are mentally stuck in a loop of resentment or humiliation.

The Protocol:

1. Take a piece of paper and a black pen.
2. The Purge: Write down every thought that is tormenting you. Be raw. Be ugly. Use profanity if you need to. Write down what you wish you could say to the person who hurt you. Get the poison out of the mind and onto the paper. Do not censor yourself.
3. The Witness: Once finished, hold the paper. Do not re-read it (re-reading re-ingests the poison). Look at it as an object separate from you.
4. The Burning: Go to a safe place (a sink, a fire bowl, or outside). Light the paper with a match.
5. The Transmutation: Watch the fire consume the ink. Watch the solid structure of the paper turn into formless smoke.
   - *Visualization:* As the smoke rises, visualize your attachment to these thoughts leaving your energy field. See the energy returning to you, purified.
6. The Cleanse: Wash your hands with cold water. Splash your face. It is done. The debt is paid.

Conclusion Of Chapter 8

Lanka is burning. The message is delivered. The power of the enemy is broken. Hanuman leaps back across the ocean. The return journey is not a spy mission; it is a victory lap. He roars like a thundercloud. The Vanaras on the southern shore hear him and they know: Victory. He lands. He does not brag. He goes straight to Angada and Jambavan. They ask: *"Did you see her?"* He says one word: *"Seen. (Drishta)."*

Now, they must return to Rama. They must deliver the news that will launch a thousand ships. And we must enter the final phase of our journey. Chapter 9: The Sanjeevani Mindset. We will learn what happens when the war actually begins, and how to handle the impossible pressure of saving a life when the sun is rising against you.

CHAPTER 9: THE SANJEEVANI MINDSET

9.1 The Impossible Deadline

The war for Dharma is not a parade; it is a slaughterhouse. We often romanticize the battle between Rama and Ravana as a sterile, symbolic conflict between Good and Evil. We imagine polished armor and poetic speeches. But the scriptures describe a scene of absolute, visceral carnage. The ground of Lanka is soaked in a mud made of dust and blood. The air is thick with the copper smell of death and the screams of the dying. And in the middle of this chaos, a catastrophe strikes that threatens to end the war before it is truly won.

Lakshmana, the beloved brother of Rama, the very spine of the army, is struck. He is not hit by an arrow or a club. He is struck by the *Shakti* weapon of Indrajit. The *Shakti* is not a conventional weapon of war. It is a mystical projectile, charged with dark mantras, designed to do one specific thing: drain the *Prana* (life force) from the soul. It does not just damage the tissue; it extinguishes the inner light.

Lakshmana falls. His pulse fades. His golden skin turns the color of ash. The invincible warrior, who stood against thousands, lies motionless in the dirt. For the first time in the epic, Rama—the Avatar of the Godhead, the Stoic King, the Mariyada Purushottam—breaks down. He falls to his knees beside his brother. He weeps. The morale of the Vanara army collapses instantly. If Lakshmana dies, Rama will not fight. If Rama does not fight, the universe belongs to Ravana. The timeline of history hangs by a thread.

The physician Sushena is called from the enemy camp (a testament to the ethics of the time). He examines the wound. He checks the pulse. He looks at the stars. And then, he delivers a diagnosis that sounds less like a cure and more like a death sentence: *"There is only one hope. The Sanjeevani herb. It possesses the power to reverse death. But it does not grow here. It grows on the Dronagiri mountain in the Himalayas. It must be applied before the sun rises. If the first ray of the sun touches his body before the herb touches his lips, he is lost."*

Let us pause and look at the brutal logistics of this problem.

1. The Distance: Lanka (modern Sri Lanka) to the Dronagiri range (in the Himalayas) is roughly 2,500 miles. That is a 5,000-mile round trip.
2. The Time: It is already past midnight. The sun will rise in a few hours.
3. The Target: The herb is rare, specific, and grows in a dense alpine forest.

It is an Impossible Deadline. In the corporate world, we talk about "tight turnarounds" or "Q4 crunches." In the ICU, doctors talk about the "Golden Hour." But this is beyond both. This is a task designed by destiny to fail. The collective mind of the army freezes. Jambavan is old. Angada is wounded. Rama is in grief. There is only one being capable of this velocity. Hanuman.

The Psychology Of The Pressure Cooker

This moment—standing over the dying body of a loved one, with the clock ticking down to zero—is the ultimate test of the Hanuman Consciousness. When faced with an impossible deadline, the human nervous system typically reacts in one of two ways.

1. The Freeze (Tamas): The magnitude of the task paralyzes the mind. We look at the distance (5,000 miles) and the time (3 hours), and the logical mind calculates the probability of success: Zero. Despair sets in. We say, *"It's too far. It can't be done. Why bother trying? Let us just accept the loss."* This is the response of *Tamas*—inertia disguised as realism. It is the voice that says, "It is what it is."

2. The Panic (Rajas): The adrenaline floods the system. We run around frantically. We scream at subordinates. We drive fast but miss the turn. We act busy, but we are not effective. This is the response of *Rajas*—passion without precision. We burn energy, but we do not move the needle.

Hanuman represents the third option: Sattva (Lucidity) in Motion. Watch his reaction in the scripture. He does not argue with the physician. He does not ask for a feasibility study. He does not negotiate for more time. He does not look at Rama and ask, *"Are you sure?"* He simply expands his body. He bows to Rama. And he launches.

Hanuman understands a fundamental truth about high-stakes anxiety that modern psychology is only just beginning to map: Panic is a choice. Focus is a discipline. The pressure cooker is not external; it is internal. The distance to the Himalayas is a physical fact. The *fear* of the distance is a psychological choice. Hanuman enters the "Zero State." He deletes the "fear of failure" from his operating system. He realizes that looking at the clock will not stop the sun. Only moving faster than the sun will stop the sun.

The Relativity Of Time And Presence

How does he do it? How does he cover that distance? Physically, he uses *Vayu-Vega* (the speed of the wind). But metaphysically, he applies the Relativity of Presence. Albert Einstein taught us that time is relative to speed. The faster an object moves through space, the slower it moves through time. Hanuman applies this literally. But he also applies it spiritually.

When you are totally absorbed in the task—when you are in the deepest state of Flow (*Samadhi*)—time disappears. Think of a moment when you were deeply engrossed in your work, or in art, or in love. You looked up, and hours had passed in what felt like minutes. The reverse is also true. When you are suffering, when you are waiting, seconds feel like hours.

The "Tick-Tock" of anxiety comes from Time-Binding. We bind ourselves to the future result. *"What if Lakshmana dies? What if I am late? What if I fail?"* This mental projection into the future creates the sensation of "running out of time." Hanuman disconnects from the *Fruit* of the action (The Consequence) and merges completely with the *Action* itself. He does not think about the destination. He does not think about the dying prince. He *becomes* the Flight. He becomes the Velocity. In that state of total union with the mission, the friction of doubt is removed. And when friction is removed, speed becomes infinite.

The Burnout Trap Vs. The Service Engine

In our modern lives, we often face "Impossible Deadlines." The project is due tomorrow. The funding is running out. The crisis is peaking. We usually respond with "Burnout Energy"—we grind, we push, we use stimulants, we abuse our bodies. And eventually, we crash. Hanuman generates massive output without burnout. How? Because his fuel source is different. Burnout comes from the ego trying to control the outcome. *"I must do this so I look good/don't get fired."* The Ego has a small battery. Hanuman's fuel is *Bhakti* (Devotion). *"I must do this because I love Rama."* Love is a renewable energy source. It is nuclear. When you shift your internal narrative from *"I have to do this"* (Pressure) to *"I get to serve through this"* (Privilege), the biology changes. Cortisol drops. Dopamine and Endorphins rise. You can run for thousands of miles without fatigue because you are not running; you are being pulled.

Hanuman flies North. The stars blur. The ocean becomes a puddle. The earth becomes a spinning ball. He is racing the sun. And because his heart is full of the Sun of Suns (Rama), he is winning.

9.2 Lifting the Mountain (Extreme Ownership)

Hanuman reaches the Dronagiri mountain range in the Himalayas. The air is crisp and cold. The silence of the peaks is a stark contrast to the noise of the battlefield he left behind. The mountain is covered in a lush, glowing tapestry of medicinal flora. He lands. He scans the slopes. He is looking for the *Sanjeevani*—the specific herb described by Sushena. It is supposed to glow. It is supposed to look a certain way.

But here lies the second, and perhaps greater, obstacle: Ambiguity. The demons, anticipating this mission, have used their sorcery (*Maya*) to mask the true nature of the herbs. Or perhaps, simply the biodiversity of the Himalayas is overwhelming. Hanuman looks at the plants. There are thousands of them. They all seem to glow in the moonlight. *Vishalyakarani* (the healer of wounds) looks exactly like *Sandhanakarani* (the healer of skin). The life-giving herb looks suspiciously like the poisonous nightshade.

Hanuman is a warrior, not a botanist. He has the strength to crush worlds, but he lacks the specific domain expertise to identify a leaf. He stands there, in the silence of the snow, with the clock ticking in his head. The sun is preparing to rise in the East. He can feel the heat of the approaching dawn.

This is the moment of Analysis Paralysis. It is the moment the CEO stares at the spreadsheet, unable to decide which strategy to pick. It is the moment the surgeon hesitates between two arteries. The mind begins to loop:

- *"If I pick the wrong one, Lakshmana dies."*
- *"If I pick a poisonous one, I kill him myself."*
- *"If I go back to Lanka to ask, I lose too much time, and he dies."*
- *"If I stay here searching, the sun rises, and he dies."*

Most people would freeze here. They would let perfectionism kill the mission. They would return empty-handed and say, *"I'm sorry, the instructions were unclear. I didn't want to make a mistake."* They would prioritize Self-Protection over Result-Production.

The Solution Of Totality

Hanuman applies the logic of the "Zero Mind." He realizes that the *specific* answer is hidden, but the *context* is available. He thinks: *"I do not know which specific herb is the Sanjeevani. But I know for a fact that the Sanjeevani is on this mountain. Therefore, the mountain contains the solution. If I cannot separate the solution from the container, I will take the container."*

He does not pick a leaf. He digs his hands—hands that are hard as diamonds—into the base of the mountain. He invokes his *Mahima Siddhi* (The power to become infinitely large). He expands until his head touches the stratosphere. He groans with the effort of a thousand elephants. He cracks the tectonic plates. The earth shakes. The yetis and the sages meditating in the caves open their eyes in shock. With a roar of *Jai Shri Ram*, he rips the entire Dronagiri mountain—millions of tons of rock, soil, trees, snow, and herbs—off the face of the earth. He balances it on his left palm. And he takes off.

This is the spiritual definition of Extreme Ownership. Extreme Ownership means you stop making excuses about "lack of information," "ambiguity," or "lack of resources." If you cannot bring the specific solution, you bring the whole ecosystem. It is the audacity to say: *"I will not let the details stop the destiny."*

- In Business: If you don't know which specific file the client needs and they aren't answering the phone, you don't wait. You send the whole folder, the summary, and the raw data. You cover all bases.
- In Crisis: If you don't know which strategy will work, you execute all three strategies simultaneously.
- In Leadership: If you don't know the answer, you don't stall. You bring the person who does.

Imperfect Action Vs. Perfect Inaction

Let us look at the "Mountain Strategy" critically. It was inelegant. It was messy. It was ecologically disruptive (he moved a mountain!). It was inefficient (carrying millions of tons for a few grams of herbs). But it was Effective. Hanuman understood a rule that most high-performers forget: In a crisis, elegance is vanity. Effectiveness is Dharma.

We are often paralyzed by the need to be "right" or "precise." We want to use a scalpel when the situation demands a bulldozer. Hanuman teaches us that it is better to be imperfectly active than perfectly paralyzed. He chose the path of "Over-delivery." He didn't just bring the herb; he brought the soil, the roots, the worms, and the rocks. He removed the variable of "Choice" from the equation. He shifted the burden of identification from himself (the carrier) back to Sushena (the expert).

This is a masterstroke of delegation and humility. *"I am not the doctor. I am the transport. I will not pretend to be the doctor. I will just make sure the doctor has everything he could possibly need."*

9.3 The Speed of Service (Vega)

Now, visualize the return journey. Hanuman is flying south. But the physics have changed. He is no longer just a body slicing through the air. He is carrying a geological formation on one hand. The aerodynamics are terrible. The weight is crushing. The gravitational drag is immense. And the sun is racing him. The eastern horizon is turning pink.

This is the test of Vega—Speed. But in the spiritual lexicon of the *Hanuman Chalisa* (where he is called *Vega-Bandan*), speed is not just velocity; it is Urgency. It is the quality of *Seva* (Service) that refuses to delay.

There is a tragic and beautiful moment in the return journey (found in the *Ramcharitmanas*) that tests this urgency. As Hanuman flies over Ayodhya (Rama's capital), the shadow of the mountain falls over the city. Bharata, Rama's brother who is ruling as a regent, sees this massive, shapeless shadow. He assumes it is a demon bringing a weapon to destroy Ayodhya. Bharata shoots an arrow—a mantra-infused projectile. It strikes Hanuman. Hanuman, caught off guard, falls. He spirals down and crashes to the earth, the mountain teetering in his hand. He lies in the dust, groaning, *"Rama... Rama..."*

Bharata rushes to the fallen figure. He hears the name of his brother. He realizes his catastrophic mistake. He weeps, holding Hanuman's head. *"I have shot the servant of my Lord. I have doomed Lakshmana."* Bharata, desperate to fix his mistake, offers a supernatural solution. He says: *"Hanuman, climb onto my arrow. I will fire it towards Lanka. My arrow travels faster than the mind. It will get you there instantly."*

This is the temptation of the Shortcut. Hanuman is tired. He is wounded. He is carrying a mountain. The offer of a "magic bullet" ride seems perfect. But Hanuman refuses. He stands up, blood dripping from his wound. He lifts the mountain again. He says: *"O Bharata, I cannot use your arrow. Your arrow is powered by mechanics and mantras. My wings are powered by Love. Mechanical speed has a limit; Devotional speed has no limit. If I ride your arrow, I am dependent on the arrow. I must depend only on Rama. I will fly."*

Love Does Not Wait

This brings us to the core insight of this section: Urgency is a Love Language. We often think of patience as a virtue. But in service, patience can be a vice. When you love someone, you do not make them wait. When your child is sick, you drive fast. You don't obey the speed limit of "comfort." When your lover calls, you answer instantly. Delay is a sign of lukewarm devotion.

Hanuman's speed is not born of adrenaline; it is born of Empathy. He feels Lakshmana's pain in his own body. He feels Rama's grief in his own heart. Because the boundary between "Me" and "You" has dissolved (The Zero State), your emergency is my emergency. In the corporate world, we procrastinate because we are detached from the outcome. We treat the deadline as a bureaucratic rule. But if you treated the deadline as a matter of life and death—as a service to someone you love—procrastination would vanish.

Hanuman launches himself back into the sky, bleeding but unbroken. He arrives in Lanka just as the first sliver of the sun begins to crest the horizon. He blocks the sun with the mountain (or with his own size). He lands in the middle of the battlefield. Sushena runs to the mountain. He finds the herb instantly. He crushes it. Lakshmana inhales the fumes. The color returns to his cheeks. His eyes flutter open. He sits up. The army roars. Rama smiles, tears streaming down his face. The sun rises, but the Son of the Wind has won the race.

9.4 Sadhana: The "Whatever It Takes" Protocol

The "Sanjeevani Mindset" is the ability to deliver the result regardless of the obstacles. It is the shift from "Effort-based" living ("I tried my best") to "Result-based" living ("It is done"). Here is the protocol to install this operating system into your daily life.

Practice 1: The "No Excuses" Audit (Vak-Tapas)

Most of our communication is polluted with "Reasons." *"I couldn't finish the report because the internet was slow." "I was late because the traffic was bad."* Reasons are valid to the Ego, but they are zero to the Reality. The Reality only cares if the mountain is there or not.

The Protocol: For the next 7 days, take a vow of "Zero Reasons." If you fail to deliver a task:

1. Do not explain "Why." (Unless specifically asked for a root cause analysis).
2. Simply say: *"I did not deliver. Here is the new ETA. Here is how I am fixing it."*
3. Observe the Burn: The Ego wants to explain. It wants to say, *"It wasn't my fault; it was the circumstance."* It craves validation.
4. Deny the Ego that relief. Sit in the fire of non-delivery. This fire will burn the habit of excuse-making and force your brain to find "Mountain Moves" next time to avoid the pain.

Practice 2: The "Bring The Mountain" Drill (Contextual Over-Delivery)

This is a problem-solving heuristic for when you are stuck in ambiguity. When you face a vague problem and don't know the specific answer:

The Protocol:

1. Stop Analyzing: Give yourself exactly 5 minutes to find the specific "herb" (the precise answer).

2. The Trigger: If you can't find it in 5 minutes, stop digging. Trigger the "Mountain Mode."
3. Scale Up: Ask, *"What is the 'Mountain' here? What is the container that holds the answer?"*
   - *Scenario:* Your boss asks for a specific metric, but the data is messy.
   - *The Herb:* Trying to clean the data perfectly (might take too long).
   - *The Mountain:* Send the raw data, the cleaned subset, an alternative proxy metric, and a qualitative analysis of the trend. Over-deliver the context so the decision can still be made.
   - *Scenario:* You are hosting a dinner and don't know the dietary restrictions of a guest.
   - *The Mountain:* Prepare a vegan option, a gluten-free option, and a meat option. Cover the base.
4. Execute: Deliver the Volume.
   - *Note:* Use this sparingly. It is high-energy. But in a crisis, it saves the day.

Practice 3: The Urgency Visualization (The Sun Is Rising)

To cure procrastination, you must mortalize the deadline. You must make the stakes visceral.

The Protocol:

1. Select a task you have been delaying (The Sanjeevani).
2. Close your eyes.
3. Visualize the Consequence: Do not visualize the paperwork. Visualize the *pain* caused to others by the delay.
   - *Who suffers if this is late?*
   - *Who is waiting for this 'Sanjeevani'?*
   - *See 'Lakshmana' (your project/team/goal) dying.*
4. Visualize the Sun: See the light creeping over the hori-

zon. Feel the heat. Realize that time is not a renewable resource.

5. The Shift: Feel the "Good Anxiety"—not the anxiety of fear, but the anxiety of service.
6. The Launch: Open your eyes and work for 25 minutes (Pomodoro) with the intensity of Hanuman flying. Do not stop until the timer rings.

Lakshmana is saved. The impossible has been achieved. Hanuman did not just save a life; he saved the timeline of the universe. He showed us that when you combine Focus, Ownership, and Urgency, miracles become standard operating procedure. He taught us that the world bends to the will of the one who refuses to accept "No" as an answer.

But the war is not over. The greatest villain still stands. Ravana is alive. And now that his army is destroyed, his son is dead, and his brother is saved, Ravana is cornered. And a cornered demon is the most dangerous thing in creation.

In the next and final chapter, we move to the finale. Chapter 10: The Open Heart. We will see the end of the war, the coronation of the King, and the final, ultimate revelation of who Hanuman truly is. We will witness the moment where the Warrior becomes the Mystic. We will tear open the chest.

CHAPTER 10: THE HUMBLE VICTOR

10.1 The Paradox of Power

The war is over. The dust has settled on the battlefield of Lanka. The silence that follows the roar of battle is heavy and profound. Ravana, the terrifying ten-headed ego who held the universe in a chokehold, lies dead. His golden city is charred. His invincible army is scattered. Standing amidst the wreckage is the architect of this victory. He is not the King (Rama). He is not the Prince (Lakshmana). He is the Vanara who leaped, who burned, who carried mountains, and who killed giants.

By all worldly metrics, this is Hanuman's moment. In a modern context, this is the CEO who turned the company around. This is the athlete who scored the winning goal. This is the general who won the war. The natural psychological progression at this stage is Inflation. The ego wants to claim the credit. It wants to stand on the podium and say, *"I did this."*

But look at Hanuman. As the victory drums sound, he does not stand on the chest of the fallen enemy. He does not demand a crown. He does not ask for territory. He goes to Rama, folds his hands in *Anjali Mudra*, and bows his head so low that it touches the earth. When asked who he is by the liberated sages, he does not say, *"I am the Great Hero."* He says, *"Dasoham Kosalendrasya." "I am the servant of the King of Kosala."*

This is the Paradox of Power: The strongest being in the universe is also the most humble. In the West, we often mistake humility for weakness. We think of the "humble" person as someone who lacks confidence or self-esteem. But the humility of Hanuman is not born of low self-worth; it is born of high reality-testing. He knows the physics of power: The current does not belong to the wire. The wire carries the electricity, but if the wire thinks *it* is the source of the power, it will burn out. Hanuman knows he is the wire. Rama is the current.

The Fruit-Laden Branch

There is a beautiful proverb in the agricultural traditions of India: *"The empty branch points upwards to the sky in arrogance. The fruit-laden branch bows down to the earth in gratitude."*

When you are empty of substance, your ego stands tall. You post about your hustle; you brag about your plans. You are rigid. But when you are full of substance—when you have actually lifted the mountain, when you have actually burned the city—you naturally bow. Why? Because the weight of the achievement grounds you. You realize how many factors had to align for this success to happen. You realize that you were just a conduit for a force much larger than your small self.

Hanuman bows not because he is trained to be polite, but because he is heavy with *Bhakti*. He understands that "Posturing" is a waste of energy. The lion does not need to roar to prove he is a lion; his presence is enough. The quiet confidence of Hanuman stands in stark contrast to the loud arrogance of Ravana. Ravana spent his life telling everyone how great he was. Hanuman spent his life showing everyone how great Rama is. Ravana is dead. Hanuman is immortal.

The Danger Of Victory

Victory is often more dangerous than defeat. Defeat humbles

you. It forces you to introspect. It breaks the shell of the ego. Victory feeds the ego. It validates your illusions. It whispers, *"You are special. You are invincible."* This is why so many high-performers crash after their biggest wins. The "I" becomes too heavy to carry.

Hanuman survives the toxic radiation of success by wearing the lead suit of Dasya Bhakti (Devotion of Servitude). He deflects the praise. When the Vanaras cheer for him, he points to Rama. He essentially says: *"Do not look at the arrow; look at the Archer. I am just the tip that pierced the target. The momentum came from Him."*

10.2 Rejecting the Pearls

We now move to the famous Coronation Scene (*Pattabhisheka*) in Ayodhya. The atmosphere is festive. The exile is over. Rama is on the throne. It is time for the distribution of rewards. Rama gives priceless gifts to the kings and warriors who supported him. Then, Sita takes off her own necklace—a string of celestial pearls, glowing with the light of the moon. She looks for the most deserving person in the assembly. She gives it to Hanuman.

The court watches in awe. This is the ultimate validation. To wear the Queen's necklace is to be marked as the favorite. Hanuman takes the necklace. He looks at it with deep curiosity. Then, he does something that shocks the civilized court. He puts a pearl in his mouth and crunches it. He spits out the dust. He takes the next pearl, bites it, inspects the fragments, and throws them away. One by one, he destroys the priceless jewels.

The Value System Of The Mystic

The ministers are horrified. They whisper, *"Look at this stupid monkey. He does not know the value of gems. You can take the beast out of the forest, but you cannot take the forest out of the beast."* A general stands up and shouts, *"Hanuman! Are you mad? You are destroying the gift of the Mother. This is an insult!"*

Hanuman stops. He looks at the general with eyes of absolute clarity. *"I am looking for Rama,"* he says simply. *"I cracked the pearl to see if the Name of Rama was written inside. But it was empty. It was just stone. What use do I have for a stone that does not hold my Lord?"*

This scene is a radical deconstruction of Material Value. To the world, the pearl is valuable because it is rare, expensive, and confers status. To Hanuman, value is binary:

1. Does it vibrate with the Truth (Rama)?
2. Or is it dead matter?

If it does not have "Rama" in it—if it does not possess the frequency of the Divine—it is weight. It is clutter. It is trash. Hanuman applies the Vedantic logic of *Neti Neti* (Not this, Not this). He bites the wealth of the world and finds it tasteless.

The Diamond vs. The Stone

This is a confrontation between the Economic Mind and the Devotional Mind. The Economic Mind hoards things because they have market value. We keep jobs we hate because they pay well. We maintain friendships that are toxic because they are "strategic." We cling to pearls that are empty inside. The Devotional Mind is ruthless. It asks: *"Does this bring me closer to the Source?"*

- If the job does not serve your Dharma, it is just a stone. Spit it out.
- If the fame does not amplify the Truth, it is just noise. Spit it out.

Hanuman teaches us that we must define our own value system against the market. Just because the world calls it a "pearl" doesn't mean you have to wear it. If it feels heavy on your neck, if it doesn't ring with the sound of your own soul's purpose, have the courage to break it.

10.3 Daso'ham: The Identity of the Servant

The general challenges Hanuman further. *"You expect everything to have Rama in it? You are wearing a body. Your skin, your bones, your fur—do they have Rama in them? Or is your body also just a stone?"* This leads to the philosophical climax of the chapter.

Hanuman does not give a lecture on non-duality. He lives it. But before we get to the physical proof (which we will explore in the final chapter), we must understand his internal software. His operating system is Daso'ham.

- *Das* = Servant
- *Aham* = I am *"I am a Servant."*

In the modern world, "servant" is a dirty word. It implies inferiority, slavery, and lack of agency. We all want to be "Leaders," "Kings," and "Bosses." But in the spiritual lexicon, *Dasya* is the highest form of freedom. Why? Because the Master carries the burden.

The Burden Of Doership (Kartrutva)

The greatest source of stress in human life is the feeling of Doership (*Kartrutva*). *"I have to make this happen." "I have to fix this." "It's all on me."* This is the Atlas Complex—carrying the weight of the world on your shoulders. It leads to anxiety, burnout, and ego-inflation.

When Hanuman adopts the identity of the Servant, he hands the weight of the world to Rama.

- The war? That is Rama's war.
- The ocean? That is Rama's ocean.

- The victory? That is Rama's victory. Hanuman is merely the Instrument (*Nimitta-matram*).

Think of a pen. The pen does not worry about what is being written. It does not stress about spelling errors. It does not take pride in the poetry. The pen simply keeps its ink flowing and allows the writer to move it. Because the pen claims no credit, it carries no burden. Hanuman is the Pen. Rama is the Poet.

Dualism As A Tool For Intimacy

Philosophically, this is the path of Dvaita (Dualism). In *Advaita* (Non-Dualism), you say *"I am God."* This is the ultimate truth, but it can be dry. In *Dvaita*, you say *"I am His."* This maintains a slight separation—the distance required for a relationship. You cannot hug yourself. You need "The Other" to experience love. Hanuman chooses to remain a servant not because he is ignorant of his divinity, but because he craves the Intimacy of Service. He wants to massage Rama's feet. He wants to fetch water. He wants to fight battles. He realizes that the joy of serving God is greater than the joy of *being* God.

This identity of *Daso'ham* liberates him from the ego. If you insult a servant, he doesn't take it personally; he refers you to the Master. If you praise a servant, he doesn't take it personally; he refers you to the Master. He is transparent. He is free.

10.4 Sadhana: The Practice of Invisible Service

How do we practice *Dasya Bhakti* in a world that worships the ego? We do it through Karma Yoga—the yoga of action. But specifically, the practice of *Invisible Service.*

Most of our service is transactional. We do good to look good. We donate to get a plaque. We help to get a "Thank You." Hanuman does not wait for the thank you. He often acts in the shadows (like in the Ashoka Vatika before the reveal).

Practice 1: The Secret Agent Of Good

The Protocol: For the next 7 days, perform one act of service daily that no one knows about.

- Clean the shared kitchen at work when no one is looking.
- Pay for the coffee of the person behind you anonymously.
- Fix something broken in your house without telling your spouse.

The Rule: If you tell anyone, the "spiritual points" are voided. The ego has eaten the fruit. The Insight: Observe the feeling of holding the secret. The ego will scream to share it: *"Look what I did!"* Suppress that urge. Let the energy of the good deed build up inside you. This internal pressure converts into *Ojas* (spiritual radiance). You are training yourself to work for the approval of the Inner Witness (Rama), not the outer audience.

Practice 2: The "Instrument" Visualization

Use this before starting any high-pressure task (a presentation, a difficult conversation, a creative project).

The Protocol:

1. Sit for 1 minute.
2. Visualize yourself as a hollow bamboo reed.
3. Visualize the task as a song that needs to be played.
4. Say silently: *"I am the flute. You are the breath. Play through me."*
5. Relinquish the Result: Say: *"The outcome of this action belongs to You. The success is Yours. The failure is Yours. I am only responsible for the effort."*

This removes performance anxiety. You are not performing; you are being played.

Practice 3: The "Daso'ham" Audit

When you feel stressed or overwhelmed, do a quick audit: *"Who is carrying this burden?"*

- Is it "Me" (the small ego)?
- Or is it "The Servant"?

Shift the identity. *"I am just the manager of this life; I am not the owner." Service is the rent we pay for the privilege of breath.* But the Owner is responsible for the repairs. Hand the repair bill to Rama.

Conclusion Of Chapter 10

Hanuman has rejected the pearls. He has declared his identity. He has shown that the Victor is merely the Vehicle. But the assembly is still skeptical. The general still doubts. *"You say you are a servant, but where is the Master? Is He just a concept in your head?"*

Hanuman knows it is time for the final proof. Words are no longer enough. He must show them the anatomy of a devotee. He must show them that the Master is not just in the temple; He is in the tissue.

In the final chapter, we will witness the event that defines the iconography of Hanuman forever. We enter Chapter 11: The Open Heart. We will see the tearing of the chest, the revelation of the internal throne, and the final choice to remain an Immortal (*Chiranjeevi*) upon the earth.

CHAPTER 11: THE OPEN HEART

11.1 Tearing the Chest (The Ultimate Reveal)

The war is over. The fourteen years of exile are complete. The arrows have been put back in their quivers, the wounds have been healed by the *Sanjeevani*, and the blood has been washed from the earth of Lanka. We are no longer in the dark, predator-filled forests of Dandaka, nor in the burning, golden ruins of the demon city. We have returned to Ayodhya—the City of No Conflict.

The atmosphere is electric with a joy that borders on madness. Millions of oil lamps (*Deepavali*) are lit, turning the dark moon night into a blazing day. The air is thick with the scent of camphor, jasmine, and sandalwood. The streets are paved with flower petals. Rama, the Prince who became a Beggar, the Warrior who became a King, finally sits on the Golden Throne. Beside him sits Sita, the Mother of the Universe, her eyes radiating a peace that has seen the fires of hell and survived.

This is the Pattabhisheka—the Coronation. It is the moment every character in the epic has fought for, bled for, and waited for. It is the restoration of Dharma. To reward his loyal army, Rama begins the ceremony of gift-giving. He hands out kingdoms to the kings. He gives Angada armlets of diamond. He crowns Vibhishana as the King of Lanka. He embraces Sugriva and gives him a garland of celestial gold. Everyone is receiving their due. The currency of the world—gold, land, power—is flowing freely.

Then, Sita takes off her own necklace. It is a string of rare, celestial pearls given to her by the Wind God, Vayu, and guarded by her through the long years of imprisonment. It is priceless. It represents the grace of the Divine Mother. She holds it in her hand, the pearls shimmering in the lamp-light, and she looks around the court. She is looking for the one who deserves the highest honor. Her eyes stop on Hanuman. The court goes silent. This is the ultimate validation. To receive the personal necklace of the Queen is to be elevated above all kings and generals. She places the pearls around Hanuman's neck. The court erupts in applause.

What happens next is the most shocking, confusing, and violent moment in the entire epic. It is the moment where the logic of the world crashes against the logic of the mystic.

Hanuman takes the necklace off. He holds it up to his ear. He shakes it. He squints at it with deep, animal scrutiny. Then, he brings a pearl to his mouth and crunches it between his teeth. The sound echoes through the silent hall. He spits out the dust. He looks at the powder with disgust. He takes the next pearl, bites it, cracks it open, looks inside, and throws it away. One by one, he destroys the priceless jewels. He reduces the gift of the Goddess to a pile of grit on the palace floor.

The Outrage Of The Ego

The silence of the court turns into a gasp of horror. The ministers are appalled. The generals are insulted. *"Look at this stupid monkey!"* they whisper. *"He does not know the value of gems. You can dress a beast in silk, but he remains a beast. He has insulted the Queen. He has insulted the King."*

One of the generals stands up, his face red with indignation. *"Hanuman! Have you lost your mind? These are not ordinary stones. These are gifts from the Mother of the Universe. They are worth more than your entire life. Why are you destroying them?"*

Hanuman stops. He holds the last remaining pearl in his hand. He looks at the general with eyes of absolute innocence and absolute fire. *"I am looking for Rama,"* he says. *"I cracked the pearl to see if the sound of Rama's name was inside. But it was empty. It was silent. It was just stone. What use do I have for a stone that does not hold my Lord?"*

The general laughs, a cold, cynical laugh. *"Do you expect everything to have Rama in it? You are wearing a body. Your skin, your bones, your fur—do they have Rama in them? Or is your devotion just a show? Is it just a performance to get a seat near the throne?"*

The Vajra Of Vulnerability

This is the challenge. It is the challenge the world throws at every mystic, every seeker, every person who dares to live by a higher code. *"Prove it." "Show us that your spirituality is real." "Show us that you are not just another hypocrite wearing the mask of piety."*

Hanuman does not argue. He does not quote scripture. He does not offer a philosophical rebuttal about the omnipresence of Brahman. He stands in the center of the hall. The festive lights reflect in his eyes. He closes his eyes for a second, tuning into the frequency of the Zero State. He drops into the silence beneath the noise. Then, he digs his sharp, diamond-hard claws into the center of his own chest.

With a roar that shakes the pillars of the palace, he tears his chest open.

It is a gruesome image. It violates our instinct for self-preservation. It is biological suicide. But in the logic of the *Hanuman Consciousness*, it is the only rational act. Blood does not flow. Light flows. There is no gore. There is only Glory.

There, in the cavern of his heart—the *Hridayakasha*—sitting on a throne of living light, are the images of Sita and Rama. They are not static images. They are not paintings. They are alive. They are breathing. And the court hears it. From every cell of Hanuman's body, from the marrow of his bones, from the fibers of his muscles, a sound is emanating. It is not a voice; it is a vibration. *Rama... Rama... Rama...* The sound is deafening. It fills the hall. It drowns out the music. It drowns out the doubts. It is the sound of the Universe humming the name of its Source.

The court falls to its knees. Rama himself descends from the throne. Tears stream down the face of God. He embraces Hanuman, closing the wound with his own hand, healing the tear with a touch. Hanuman stands revealed. He is not a monkey. He is a living temple.

The Psychology Of Radical Transparency

What does this moment mean for us? Why is it the climax of the book? It teaches us the concept of Radical Transparency.

Most of us live two lives. We have a Public Life—the pearls we wear, the titles we hold, the smiles we fake, the photos we post. This is the "Mask." It is polished, acceptable, and safe. And we have a Private Life—the thoughts we hide, the desires we suppress, the shadows we deny, the judgments we hold. This is the "Shadow." We are opaque. We have a "Chest" that is locked tight. We are terrified that if people saw what was really inside us—our insecurities, our fears, our mess—they would reject us. We spend 90% of our energy protecting the lock on the chest.

Hanuman has No Secrets. The outside is the servant; the inside is the Master. But there is no discrepancy between them. The tearing of the chest is the ultimate act of vulnerability. It is saying: *"Look. I have nothing to hide. Cut me anywhere, and you will find only Truth. My exterior is Rama's servant, and my interior is Rama's throne."*

This is the definition of Integrity (*Integra* = Whole). When your inner reality and your outer expression are perfectly aligned, you become invincible. Why? Because you have no "back door." You have no lies to protect. You have no image to defend. You do not need to remember what you said to whom, because you live in the Truth. You are an "Open Book." You are an Open Heart.

In the modern world, we are taught that power comes from secrecy. Corporations protect their trade secrets; governments classify their data; individuals curate their Instagram feeds to show only the highlights. We think mystery creates power. But spiritual power comes from openness. The "Hanuman Consciousness" is the state where you can stand before the universe, before your critics, before your enemies, and say: *"This is who I am. There is no discrepancy between my prayer and my practice."*

The Rejection Of Value (Neti Neti)

The breaking of the pearls is also a profound lesson in Valuation. Hanuman is described in the scriptures as *Jnaninam Agraganyam*—the Wisest of the Wise. How can the wisest being not know the value of pearls? He knows their *market* value. He knows they are worth millions. But he operates on *Soul Value.*

To the world, the pearl is precious because it is rare, shiny, and expensive. To Hanuman, the pearl is worthless because it is Silent. He is applying the Vedantic method of *Neti Neti* (Not this, Not this).

- He bites the pearl. *"Is Rama here?"* No. *"Neti."* Throw it away.
- He looks at the gold. *"Is Rama here?"* No. *"Neti."* Throw it away.

He teaches us a new metric for success. In the "Search for Zero," we stop asking, "How much does this cost?" or "what will people think of this?" We start asking: Does this vibrate with Truth?

- The Career Test: Does this job have "Rama" in it? (Is it aligned with my purpose? Does it serve the whole?) If not, it is just a stone.
- The Relationship Test: Does this relationship have "Rama" in it? (Does it help me grow? Is it based on love or transaction?) If not, it is just a stone.
- The Habit Test: Does this habit have "Rama" in it? (Does it give me energy or drain it?)

If the answer is No, then it is just a stone. It doesn't matter how expensive it is. It doesn't matter if society calls it a "pearl." It doesn't matter if everyone else is chasing it. Crack it open. Look inside. If it is empty, have the courage to throw it away. This is the ruthless discrimination (*Viveka*) of the Yogi. You must be willing to spit out the pearls of the world to protect the diamond of the soul.

11.2 Sita-Ram Within (The Theology of the Heart)

When Hanuman opens his chest, what exactly does the court see? They see Sita and Rama. But wait. Pause the scene. Sita and Rama are sitting *outside* on the golden throne, watching this happen. So, how can they be inside Hanuman at the same time?

This creates a theological paradox that shatters the linear mind.

- If Rama is God, and God is outside, who is inside?
- If Rama is inside, why did Hanuman spend the last 10 chapters serving the Rama outside?
- Is the Rama inside a reflection, or is He the Reality?

This brings us to the deepest secret of the Ramayana and the core of the "Zero" philosophy: The External Journey was a Metaphor for the Internal Discovery.

Antaryami (The Inner Controller)

In the beginning of this book (Chapter 1), we discussed the "Jambavan Effect"—the idea that we have forgotten our power. Now, at the end, we realize we haven't just forgotten our power; we have forgotten our Occupant. The body is not a house for the ego. It is not a vehicle for sensory gratification. It is a Temple for the Divine. The Sanskrit word for this is *Antaryami*—the Inner Controller.

Hanuman realizes a profound truth in this moment: The Rama he served for fourteen years—the Prince who walked in the forest, who cried for his wife, who bled in battle, who needed a bridge to cross the ocean—was the Historical Rama (*Avatar*). He was God playing a role (*Lila*) in time and space. But the Rama inside his heart is the Eternal Rama (*Atman*). The Historical Rama is limited by time. He will rule Ayodhya for 11,000 years and then leave his body. He will die. The Eternal Rama is timeless. He lives in the *Hridayakasha* (Heart Space) of the devotee forever. He was there before the birth of the body, and He will be there after its death.

Hanuman's greatness is that he never confused the two, yet he honored both. He served the Form (*Saguna*) with total dedication, knowing that it led to the Formless (*Nirguna*). He realized: *"I do not serve Rama because He is the King. I serve Rama because He is my own Self walking outside of me."* This is the bridge between Dualism (*Dvaita*) and Non-Dualism (*Advaita*).

- In the beginning: "I am His servant." (Dualism).
- In the middle: "I am His part." (Qualified Non-Dualism).
- In the end: "I am Him, and He is me." (Non-Dualism).

The Heart Cave (Guha)

In the *In Search of Zero* meditations, we often speak of the "Cave of the Heart" (*Guha*). This is not the physical pump that circulates blood. It is the spiritual center, described in the Upanishads as being "thumb-sized," located slightly to the right of the physical heart. It is the "Zero Point" of the human anatomy. It is the singularity where the individual wave merges back into the ocean.

When Hanuman tears his chest, he is physically revealing the Guha. He is showing us that the "Kingdom of Heaven" is not a geographical location. It is not Ayodhya. It is not Lanka. It is not a place you go to after you die. It is a biological reality hidden within the ribcage.

The entire war against Ravana was actually a war to clean this cave.

- Ravana represents the Ego that occupied the heart.
- The Rakshasas represent the desires and fears that cluttered the cave.
- Lanka was the body held hostage by the ego.
- The War was the process of excavation.

Now that the war is won, the Ego is dead, and the desires are burnt, the Cave is clean. And in a clean cave, the Light naturally shines. Hanuman is saying: *"Look, I have finished the work. My heart is no longer a jungle of monkeys; it is a throne room for God."*

The Union Of Shakti And Shiva

Notice that he does not just have Rama inside. He has Sita and Rama. In Tantric philosophy, you cannot have one without the other.

- Rama is Shiva (Consciousness / The Static Principle). He is the Silence. He is the Witness.
- Sita is Shakti (Energy / The Kinetic Principle). She is the

Power. She is the Flow.
- Hanuman is the Container that holds both.

This is the state of Purnata (Completeness). Many seekers have the "Rama" (Intellectual understanding of Truth). They are calm, detached, and wise. But they lack the "Sita" (The devotion, the feeling, the love). They are dry. They are brittle. Others have the "Sita" (Emotional fervor, passion, ecstatic dance). But they lack the "Rama" (Discipline, Clarity, Boundaries). They are chaotic and ungrounded.

Hanuman has integrated the Head and the Heart. He has the discipline to cross the ocean (Rama) and the devotion to weep for the Mother (Sita). He has the strength to burn a city and the tenderness to console a captive. He is the perfect Androgynous Soul—tough as a diamond (*Vajra*), soft as a flower (*Kusuma*). He carries the Father and the Mother within him. He is the Orphan who became the Heir.

The Death Of Distance

When you realize that "Sita-Ram is Within," the concept of distance dies. Throughout the book, Hanuman was traveling. He traveled to the South. He traveled to the Himalayas. He traveled to Ayodhya. Movement (*Vayu*) was his nature. But in this moment, the movement stops. Where is there to go? If the destination is inside you, then every step is an arrival.

This is the state of Sahaja Samadhi (Natural Absorption). Hanuman no longer needs to close his eyes to meditate. He no longer needs to go to a cave. He no longer needs to fly to a mountain. He can walk, talk, eat, and fight, and yet, he is always looking at the picture in his chest. He has achieved the "Walking Zero." He is in the world, but the world is not in him. Rama is in him. He has become a portable shrine. Wherever he sits, that place becomes Ayodhya. Wherever he breathes, the air becomes sanctified.

This is the promise of the Hanuman Consciousness. It promises that you do not have to leave the world to find the Truth. You do not have to become a monk. You do not have to retire to an ashram. You simply have to tear open the chest of your own ego, clean the cave of your heart, and install the Ideal there. Once the installation is complete, you are free. You are Home.

11.3 The Chiranjeevi State (The Choice to Remain)

The chest has been torn. The devotion has been proven. The paradox of the internal and external God has been resolved. But the Ramayana has one final twist—a twist that elevates Hanuman from a Devotee to a Savior.

Rama is preparing to leave. His earthly mission is complete. The demon Ravana is dead. The Dharma is restored. It is time for the Avatar to return to His eternal abode, *Vaikuntha* (The Spiritual World). Rama gathers his inner circle. He offers them the ultimate reward: Moksha (Liberation). *"Come with me,"* he says. *"Leave this plane of suffering (Mrityu-Loka). Come to the realm where there is no death, no pain, and no separation. Come and live with Me forever in eternal bliss."*

Everyone agrees. Who would refuse heaven? Who would refuse to leave the cycle of birth and death? Sugriva agrees. Angada agrees. Even the citizens of Ayodhya prepare to leave. But Hanuman stands silent. He asks Rama a strange question: *"My Lord, in your eternal abode of Vaikuntha, will you be there as Rama?"* Rama smiles. *"In Vaikuntha, I am Narayana. I am the formless absolute, or the four-armed Vishnu."* Hanuman asks again: *"And will the story of the Ramayana be recited there? Will the glory of your name be chanted?"* Rama shakes his head. *"In Vaikuntha, everything is perfect. There is no story, because there is no conflict. There is only silence and bliss."*

Hanuman steps back. He folds his hands. *"Then, my Lord, I cannot come."*

The Rejection Of Moksha

The court is stunned again. Hanuman is refusing God. He is refusing the very goal of all spiritual practice. Every Yogi meditates for Moksha. Every ascetic burns his body for Liberation. And here is Hanuman, offered a free ticket to the ultimate destination, saying "No."

He says: *"I do not want your heaven if your Name is not there. I do not want bliss if it means I cannot serve you. I choose to stay here. I choose to stay on this Earth, where there is pain, where there is death, where there is suffering. Because as long as your Name is chanted on this Earth, you are here. And where your Name is, there is my heaven."*

This is the Chiranjeevi State. *Chiram* (Long/Eternal) + *Jeevi* (Living). Hanuman becomes an Immortal. Not because he fears death, but because he loves Service more than he loves Peace.

The Bodhisattva Vow

This parallels the Bodhisattva Vow in Mahayana Buddhism. The Bodhisattva reaches the door of Nirvana (Enlightenment). But he stops. He hears the cries of suffering beings behind him. He refuses to enter Nirvana until every single blade of grass is enlightened. He turns his back on peace to face the pain of the world.

Hanuman is the original Bodhisattva. He realizes that "Going to Heaven" is a subtle form of selfishness. It is an escape. True spirituality is not about *leaving* the matrix; it is about *transforming* the matrix. Hanuman chooses to remain in the "Mud" of the material world to help the other "Lotuses" bloom.

He makes a vow: *"Wherever the name of Rama is spoken, I will be there. Wherever a devotee is in trouble, I will be there. I will sit in the corner of every temple, unnoticed, tears flowing from my eyes, protecting the faith of the weak."*

Immortality Through Presence

So, where is Hanuman now? According to the Chiranjeevi concept, he is not a mythological figure in a book. He is a living entity on this planet *right now*. He is the Guardian of the Atmosphere. He exists in the subtle ether (*Akasha*). Whenever you read this book, whenever you chant the Hanuman Chalisa, whenever you feel a surge of courage in a moment of fear—that is Him. He is not a "God" sitting on a cloud. He is a Frequency available in the atmosphere.

The Chiranjeevi State teaches us the highest level of the Hanuman Consciousness: Service is higher than Silence.

- Silence is for you. Service is for others.
- Bliss is for you. Sacrifice is for others.
- Moksha is for you. Love is for others.

The ultimate Yogi does not run away to a cave. He stays in the city. He stays in the family. He stays in the job. He remains in the world of duality to anchor the non-dual Truth. He becomes a Living Bridge between the human and the divine.

11.4 Sadhana: The Hridaya Dharana (Centering In The Heart)

We have completed the journey. We have moved from the Amnesia of Chapter 1 to the Immortality of Chapter 10. How do we seal this practice? How do we take the "Hanuman Consciousness" and make it our permanent operating system?

We end with the Hridaya Dharana—The Fixing of the Mind in the Heart. This is not just a meditation technique; it is a way of being.

The Practice: Installing The Murti

1. The Seat of Power: Sit in a comfortable posture. Spine erect. Close your eyes. Take 3 deep, slow breaths. Visualize your body as the City of Ayodhya—golden, lit with lamps, festive.

2. The Cave: Bring your attention to the center of your chest, slightly to the right of the physical heart. Visualize a small, luminous cave (*Guha*). It is quiet here. The noise of the world cannot enter.

3. The Installation: Inside this cave, visualize a golden throne. On this throne, mentally place your Ishta-Devata (Your chosen Ideal).

- It may be Rama and Sita.
- It may be Christ.
- It may be a ball of pure Light.
- It may be the word "Truth." See it clearly. See it shining with its own self-effulgent light (*Svyam-Jyoti*).

4. The Tearing: Now, perform the psychic act of Hanuman. Visualize your hands tearing open the veil of your ego that covers this cave. Say silently: *"I remove the mask. I reveal the Truth."*

5. The Offering: Every thought that arises, offer it to the Image in the cave.

- A worry comes? Offer it.
- An ambition comes? Offer it.
- A fear comes? Offer it. Say: *"This is Yours. You take care of it."*

6. The Walk: Open your eyes. As you stand up and walk, imagine

you are carrying this shrine inside you. Walk gently, so you don't disturb the Deity. Speak truth, so you don't offend the Deity. Act with courage, so you honor the Deity.

The Final Sankalpa

Let us close this book with a final Sankalpa (Vow). We do not ask for powers. We do not ask for kingdoms. We do not even ask for Moksha. We ask for the only thing Hanuman asked for.

Put your hand on your chest. Feel the beat of the heart. Repeat this vow:

"I am the Instrument. You are the Player. I am the Arrow. You are the Archer. I am the Temple. You are the Light. Use me. Burn my ego. Break my chains. Fill me with Your strength, so I may serve Your world. As long as I have breath, let it be a chant of Truth. Jai Bajrangbali. Jai Shri Ram."

CONCLUSION

The Living Bridge

We have traveled a long distance together. From the shores of doubt to the burning of Lanka, from the carrying of the mountain to the tearing of the chest. We have seen that the journey of Hanuman is actually the journey of the human soul. It begins with Amnesia (forgetting who we are). It proceeds through Action (the Leap). It is tested by Obstacles (Comfort, Ego, Shadow). It is refined by Fire (Humiliation and Anger). And it culminates in Love (The Open Heart).

The ultimate lesson of the Hanuman Consciousness is that Power is not the goal; it is the tool. Strength without devotion is dangerous (Ravana). Devotion without strength is helpless. But strength married to devotion is invincible (Hanuman).

As you close this book, do not leave the consciousness behind. The world needs more Hanumans. It needs people who are strong enough to burn the structures of injustice, yet tender enough to weep for the suffering of others. It needs leaders who lift mountains not for their own glory, but to save a brother. It needs warriors who carry the temple in their hearts.

You are the Instrument. The breath in your lungs is *Vayu*. The fire in your belly is *Agni*. The witness in your heart is *Rama*. The bridge has been built. Now, walk across it.

Jai Bajrangbali.

GLOSSARY OF SANSKRIT TERMS

- Advaita: Non-Dualism. The philosophy that there is only One Reality.
- Agni: Fire; the transformative element.
- Anima: The Siddhi (power) of becoming infinitely small.
- Antaryami: The Inner Controller; the Divine presence within the heart.
- Bhakti: Devotion; the path of love.
- Brahmacharya: Control of the senses; specifically, the conservation and transmutation of sexual energy.
- Buddhi: The Intellect; the discerning faculty of the mind.
- Chiranjeevi: Immortal; one who lives forever to serve.
- Dharma: Righteousness; duty; cosmic order.
- Dharma-Krodha: Righteous Anger; anger used to protect Dharma.
- Ekagrata: One-pointed focus.
- Guha: The Cave of the Heart; the spiritual center.
- Jitendriya: Conqueror of the senses.
- Karma Yoga: The yoga of selfless action.
- Kumbhaka: Breath retention.
- Mahima: The Siddhi of becoming infinitely large.
- Maya: Illusion; or the creative power of the Divine.
- Ojas: Spiritual vigor; the subtle energy produced by Brahmacharya.
- Prana: Life force; vital energy.
- Sadhana: Spiritual practice or discipline.
- Sankalpa: A solemn vow or resolve; intention.

- Satsang: Association with the Truth (or truth-seekers).
- Shravanam: Deep listening (to scripture or truth).
- Siddhi: Supernatural power or perfection.
- Vairagya: Detachment; dispassion.
- Vayu: The Wind God; the cosmic life force.
- Vega: Speed; momentum; urgency.

THE COMPLETE LIBRARY OF KANAV SACHDEV

Discover the Series That Calls to Your Soul

Series 1: The Manifestation Series

The Definitive 9-Stage Blueprint for Becoming the Conscious Architect of Your Life.

Book 1: Make the Law of Attraction Work for You Stop predicting your future and start scripting it. Go beyond passive wishing and learn the mechanical laws that govern how reality is actually built.

Book 2: Unlocking the Power of the Subconscious Mind Your life is running on autopilot. Learn to access the hidden operating system and rewrite the deep internal programs that are silently sabotaging your success.

Book 3: A Practical Guide to Quantum Jumping Time is an illusion. Learn to "jump" timelines and merge with the version of you who already has everything you desire right now.

Book 4: Unlocking the Power of Mantra, Yantra & Rudraksha Stop doing it all with your "willpower." Activate these ancient batteries of energy—sound, geometry, and nature—to amplify your intention a thousandfold.

Book 5: The Science of Vibrations & Frequencies Everything is energy. Learn the physics of your own aura and tune your personal frequency to the station of abundance, health, and love.

Book 6: Shadow Work & Emotional Alchemy You cannot manifest light while ignoring the dark. Journey into your shadow to find the gold hidden in your deepest wounds and turn pain into power.

Book 7: Sacred Rituals & Tantric Pathways Routine is mundane; ritual is magical. Fuse your intention with ancient Vedic ceremonies to turn your daily actions into unstoppable forces of nature.

Book 8: The 40-Day Reality Shift Don't just read about change —embody it. A rigorous 40-day boot camp of affirmations and meditations to kill the old you and birth the new identity you desire.

Book 9: Global Secrets of Creation The capstone of the series. Journey through Shamanism, Taoism, and Alchemy to discover the universal laws of creation that unite all wisdom traditions.

Series 2: In Search Of Zero

A 10-Volume Initiation into the Ultimate Nature of Reality.

Book 1: 112 Paths to Meditative Enlightenment The source code of enlightenment. 112 direct portals from Shiva to turn every breath and sensation into a doorway to the Infinite.

Book 2: A Guide to Astral Projections Why stay locked in one body? Learn the precise mechanics of leaving the physical form to explore the universe firsthand using time-tested techniques.

Book 3: Lucid Dreaming & the Multidimensional Mind Sleep is not just for rest; it's a laboratory. Wake up inside your dreams and use them to reprogram your mind while the world sleeps.

Book 4: 17 Vedic Meditation Techniques for Inner Stillness Modern stress requires ancient antidotes. Master the forgotten techniques of the sages that instantly soothe the nervous system and silence the noise.

Book 5: The Akashic Mind Your soul has a memory. Access the cosmic library to heal the ancestral trauma and karmic debts that don't belong to you, consciously rewriting your destiny.

Book 6: The Kundalini Path to Inner Alchemy You are sitting on a dormant volcano of power. Learn to safely wake the serpent energy and transform your biology from the inside out.

Book 7: The Power of Mantra & Sound Words are spells. Discover the specific sounds (Bija Mantras) that literally rearrange the molecular structure of your consciousness and clear energetic blocks.

Book 8: Tantra of the Void Emptiness is not nothing; it is the womb of everything. Enter the Shunyata and rest in the creative dark where all potential exists.

Book 9: The Mind of Shiva Drop the ego completely. Learn to view the drama of life through the detached, blissful eyes of the Creator—the ultimate state of observer-consciousness.

Book 10: The Elemental Path The final integration. Master Earth, Water, Fire, Air, and Space to become a living embodiment of the Cosmos.

Series 3: The Tantric Alchemy Series

For the Seeker Ready to Walk Through Fire and Emerge Reborn.

Book 1: The Mahāvidyā Code The Goddess is not just gentle; she is wild. Crack the code of the 10 Wisdom Goddesses to access untamed Shakti and manifest from a place of power.

Book 2: Echoes of Mahākāla Step into the presence of Bhairava. Claim the absolute fearlessness that comes when you look death in the eye and don't blink.

Book 3: Whispers of the Yakṣinīs Enter the 36 gates of the Uddamareshvara Tantra. A secret path to beauty, power, and profound inner alchemy for the dedicated adept.

Book 4: Eye of Bhairava Transform perception itself. Based on the Netra Tantra, this book teaches you to dissolve illusion and see through the fire of truth.

Book 5: The Shadow Protocol Based on the fierce Bhuta Damara Tantra. Confront the inner demons that haunt the subconscious and force them to serve your highest self.

Book 6: The Sacred Tantra From chaos to wholeness. Drawing from the Mahanirvana Tantra, this guide heals the fragmented self in the chaos of the Kali Yuga.

Series 4: The Breath Of Time And Destiny

A Cinematic Trilogy on Time, Alchemy, and Dissolution.

Book 1: The Living Clock Shatter the tyranny of the wristwatch. Discover "Time" not as a measurement, but as a living entity you can converse with and control.

Book 2: The Instant Oracle Stop guessing. Develop the razor-sharp intuition to know the answer before the question is even finished, accessing the wisdom of the moment.

Book 3: The Alchemist of Breath Structure changes when the breath changes. Use the alchemy of air (Swara) to transmute the lead of your destiny into gold.

Series 5: The God Consciousness

A 4-Part Journey into the Archetypes That Rule the Soul.

Book 1: The Hanuman Consciousness Service, Strength, Devotion. Move beyond worship and inhabit the archetype of the perfect servant of the Divine.

Book 2: The Krishna Consciousness Love, Strategy, Leela. Navigate the battlefield of life with a smile, mastering the art of divine play.

Book 3: The Shiva Consciousness Stillness, Destruction, Presence. Anchor yourself in the unshakeable silence that witnesses the creation of worlds.

Book 4: The Kali Consciousness The Void, The End, The Truth. Step beyond the clock and into the void of the destroyer to experience the final dissolution of the ego.

Series 6: Mythology & Consciousness

Transmissions of Ancient Memory.

Book 1: Katha – 108 Stories from the Vedas & Puranas Bypass the skeptical mind. Let these ancient myths act as "spiritual medicine," awakening deep memory and wisdom through the power of story.

Book 2: Katha Shakti – 108 Stories of the Divine Mother Journey to the 109 seats of the Goddess and witness the raw, creative power of the Feminine that fuels the universe.

Series 7: The Nlp Mastery Series

Unlock the Language of the Subconscious for Influence.

Book 1: Unlocking Sales Success People don't buy products; they buy trust. Learn the subconscious language that makes "Yes" the only natural answer.

Book 2: Human Potential Unlocked True leadership is resonance. Learn to lead teams not by authority, but by emotional pacing, identity design, and inner clarity.

Book 3: The Persuasion Code Negotiation is a science. Decode the neuroscience of influence to shift beliefs and shape outcomes without force.

Standalone Titles For Success

Essential Guides for the Modern Achiever.
- Procrastination No More You aren't lazy; you're just unregulated. Use neuroscience-backed strategies to break the paralysis, move from "stuck" to "unstoppable," and achieve your goals.
- Clockwork: Guide to Streamlined Business Operations Chaos is not a strategy. Build the systems that allow your business to run like a well-oiled machine—eliminating bottlenecks so it can grow with or without you.
- Global Gateway: The Complete Guide To Studying Abroad The world is your classroom. A comprehensive blueprint for the high-achiever to secure a seat at the world's top universities and launch a global career.

The Archives Of Consciousness

A Roadmap for the Soul by Kanav Sachdev
- You are holding one piece of a larger puzzle. This library is not a random collection of books; it is a connected system designed to guide you from where you are to where you are meant to be.
- Locate your current hunger below to discover your next step.

PHASE 1: THE ARCHITECT (Master Your Reality)
For the seeker who is ready to stop waiting and start commanding. If you feel stuck, limited, or powerless, start here.
-Manifestation (Book 1): Make the Law of Attraction Work for

You Stop predicting your future and start scripting it. Go beyond passive wishing and learn the mechanical laws that govern how reality is built.

-Procrastination No More: A Guide to Productivity You aren't lazy; you're just unregulated. Use neuroscience-backed strategies to break the paralysis, move from "stuck" to "unstoppable," and achieve your goals.

-Manifestation (Book 2): Unlocking the Power of the Subconscious Mind Your life is running on autopilot. Learn to access the hidden operating system and rewrite the deep internal programs that keep sabotaging your success.

-Manifestation (Book 8): The 40-Day Reality Shift Don't just read about change—embody it. A rigorous 40-day boot camp of affirmations and meditations to kill the old you and birth the new identity you desire.

-Clockwork: Guide to Streamlined Business Operations Chaos is not a strategy. Build the systems that allow your business to run like a well-oiled machine—eliminating bottlenecks so it can grow with or without you.

Phase 2: The Healer (Restore Your Soul)

For the seeker carrying heavy emotional baggage, repeating ancestral patterns, or feeling "blocked" by invisible walls.

-Manifestation (Book 6): Shadow Work & Emotional Alchemy You cannot manifest light while ignoring the dark. Journey into your shadow to find the gold hidden in your deepest wounds and turn pain into power.

-In Search of Zero (Book 5): The Akashic Mind Your soul has a memory. Access the cosmic library to heal the ancestral trauma and karmic debts that don't belong to you, consciously rewriting your destiny.

-Katha: 108 Stories from the Vedas & Puranas Bypass the skeptical mind. Let these ancient myths act as "spiritual medicine," awakening deep memory and wisdom through the power of story.

-In Search of Zero (Book 4): 17 Vedic Meditation Techniques Modern stress requires ancient antidotes. Master the forgotten techniques of the sages that instantly soothe the nervous system and silence the noise.

Phase 3: The Magician (Awaken Your Power)

For the seeker who wants to "turn up the voltage." Learn to use sound, energy, and vibration to bend reality.

-Manifestation (Book 5): The Science of Vibrations & Frequencies Everything is energy. Learn the physics of your own aura and tune your personal frequency to the station of abundance, health, and love.

-In Search of Zero (Book 7): The Power of Mantra & Sound Words are spells. Discover the specific sounds (Bija Mantras) that literally rearrange the molecular structure of your consciousness and clear energetic blocks.

--Manifestation (Book 4): Mantra, Yantra & Rudraksha Stop doing it all with your "willpower." Activate these ancient batteries of energy—sound, geometry, and nature—to amplify your intention a thousandfold.

-Manifestation (Book 7): Sacred Rituals & Tantric Pathways Routine is mundane; ritual is magical. Fuse your intention with ancient Vedic ceremonies to turn your daily actions into unstoppable forces of nature.

-In Search of Zero (Book 6): The Kundalini Path to Inner Alchemy You are sitting on a dormant volcano of power. Learn to safely wake the serpent energy and transform your biology from the inside out.

Phase 4: The Traveler (Expand Your Consciousness)

For the adventurer who knows this physical world is just a tiny fraction of what exists.

-In Search of Zero (Book 2): A Guide to Astral Projections Why stay locked in one body? Learn the precise mechanics of leaving the physical form to explore the universe firsthand using time-tested techniques.

-In Search of Zero (Book 3): Lucid Dreaming & the Multidimensional Mind Sleep is not just for rest; it's a laboratory. Wake up inside your dreams and use them to reprogram your mind while the world sleeps.

-Manifestation (Book 3): A Practical Guide to Quantum Jumping Time is an illusion. Learn to "jump" timelines and merge with the version of you who already has everything you want right now.

-The Breath of Time (Book 1): The Living Clock Shatter the tyranny of the wristwatch. Discover "Time" not as a measurement, but as a living entity you can converse with and control.

-The Breath of Time (Book 2): The Instant Oracle Stop guessing. Develop the razor-sharp intuition to know the answer before the question is even finished, accessing the wisdom of the moment.

Phase 5: The Alchemist (Walk Through Fire)

For the advanced seeker drawn to the fierce, the hidden, and the esoteric. This path is not for the timid.

-The Tantric Alchemy Series (Book 1): The Mahāvidyā Code The Goddess is not just gentle; she is wild. Crack the code of the 10 Wisdom Goddesses to access untamed Shakti and manifest from a place of power.

-The Tantric Alchemy Series (Book 5): The Shadow Protocol Based on the fierce Bhuta Damara Tantra. Confront the inner demons that haunt the subconscious and force them to serve your highest self.

-The Tantric Alchemy Series (Book 2): Echoes of Mahākāla Step into the presence of Bhairava. Claim the absolute fearlessness that comes when you look death in the eye and don't blink.

-The Breath of Time (Book 3): The Alchemist of Breath Structure changes when the breath changes. Use the alchemy of air to transmute the lead of your destiny into gold.

-Katha Shakti: 108 Stories of the Divine Mother Journey to the 109 seats of the Goddess and witness the raw, creative power of the Feminine that fuels the universe.

-The Tantric Alchemy Series (Book 3): Whispers of the Yakṣinīs Enter the 36 gates of the Uddamareshvara Tantra. A secret path to beauty, power, and profound inner alchemy for the dedicated adept.

The Tantric Alchemy Series (Book 4): Eye of Bhairava Transform perception itself. Based on the Netra Tantra, this book teaches you to dissolve illusion and see through the fire of truth.

The Tantric Alchemy Series (Book 6): The Sacred Tantra From chaos to wholeness. Drawing from the Mahanirvana Tantra, this guide heals the fragmented self in the chaos of the Kali Yuga.

Phase 6: The Mystic (Return To Source)

The final destination. For the soul seeking silence, dissolution, and the eyes of God.

-In Search of Zero (Book 1): 112 Paths to Meditative Enlightenment The source code of enlightenment. 112 direct portals from Shiva to turn every breath and sensation into a doorway to the Infinite.

-The God Consciousness Series (Book 1): The Hanuman Consciousness Service, Strength, Devotion. Move beyond worship and inhabit the archetype of the perfect servant of the Divine.

-The God Consciousness Series (Book 2): The Krishna Consciousness Love, Strategy, Leela. Navigate the battlefield of life with a smile, mastering the art of divine play.

-The God Consciousness Series (Book 3): The Shiva Consciousness Stillness, Destruction, Presence. Anchor yourself in the unshakeable silence that witnesses the creation of worlds.

-The God Consciousness Series (Book 4): The Kali Consciousness The Void, The End, The Truth. Step beyond the clock and into the void of the destroyer to experience the final dissolution of the ego.

-In Search of Zero (Book 9): The Mind of Shiva Drop the ego completely. Learn to view the drama of life through the detached, blissful eyes of the Creator.

-In Search of Zero (Book 8): Tantra of the Void Emptiness is not nothing; it is the womb of everything. Enter the Shunyata and rest in the creative dark.

-In Search of Zero (Book 10): The Elemental Path The final integration. Master Earth, Water, Fire, Air, and Space to become a living embodiment of the Cosmos.

The Leadership Vault (Master The Human World)

Strategies for influence, negotiation, and global success.

-NLP Series (Book 1): Unlocking Sales Success People don't buy products; they buy trust. Learn the subconscious language that makes "Yes" the only natural answer.

-NLP Series (Book 3): The Persuasion Code Negotiation is a science. Decode the neuroscience of influence to shift beliefs and shape outcomes without force.

-NLP Series (Book 2): Human Potential Unlocked True leadership is resonance. Learn to lead teams not by authority, but by emotional pacing, identity design, and inner clarity.

-Global Gateway: The Complete Guide To Studying Abroad The world is your classroom. A comprehensive blueprint for the high-achiever to secure a seat at the world's top universities and launch a global career.

-Manifestation (Book 9): Global Secrets of Creation The capstone of creation. Journey through Shamanism, Taoism, and Alchemy to discover the universal laws that unite all wisdom traditions.

Which voice is calling you now? Trust your intuition. The book that jumps out at you is the one your soul is asking for.

The Quantum Shortcuts

Specific Tools for Immediate Shifts

Sometimes you don't have time for the long road. You need a shift now. These specific combinations are "book prescriptions" designed to attack your biggest roadblocks from two angles simultaneously: the energetic and the practical.

For Urgent Financial Growth

The Problem: You need to generate wealth, close deals, or shift your financial reality quickly. The Solution: Combine Energetic Amplification with Psychological Influence.

-Manifestation (Book 4): Unlocking the Power of Mantra, Yantra & Rudraksha Money is energy, and you are currently blocked. Use ancient geometric (Yantra) and sonic (Mantra) tools to clear the path and magnetize your aura for abundance.

-NLP Series (Book 3): The Persuasion Code Once the energy is clear, you must close the deal. Use advanced neuroscience to bypass resistance, negotiate with power, and turn every conversation into an opportunity.

For Crushing Anxiety & Stress

The Problem: Your mind won't stop racing, you feel overwhelmed, or you are on the verge of burnout. The Solution: Combine Nervous System Regulation with Divine Detachment.

-In Search of Zero (Book 4): 17 Vedic Meditation Techniques Stop trying to "think" your way out of stress. Use these forgotten physiological switches to instantly calm the nervous system and silence the noise.

-The God Consciousness (Book 3): The Shiva Consciousness Stress comes from attachment. Step into the archetype of Shiva—the Witness—and anchor yourself in the unshakeable stillness that watches the chaos without being touched by it.

For A Total Identity Reboot

-The Problem: You feel stuck in a version of yourself that you have outgrown. You want to change your personality, habits, and life trajectory. The Solution: The Immersion Protocol.

-Manifestation (Book 8): The 40-Day Reality Shift This is not a book; it is a death-and-rebirth ceremony. Commit to this rigorous 40-day blueprint of reprogramming to kill the old identity and permanently install the new one.

For Instant Clarity & Intuition

The Problem: You are facing a major decision, you feel confused, or you need to know what the future holds. The Solution: The Breath of Time Two-Step Protocol. (Note: This power must be unlocked sequentially. You cannot use the

Oracle without the Clock.)

Step 1: The Living Clock (Book 1) First, shatter the illusion of linear time. You must learn to feel the "heartbeat" of the Living Clock before you can read it.

Step 2: The Instant Oracle (Book 2) Once attuned, use this guide to access the razor-sharp wisdom of the moment. Stop guessing and start "knowing" the answer before the question is even fully asked.

For Breaking Laziness & Inertia

The Problem: You know what to do, but you just can't get yourself to move. The Solution: Combine Brain Science with Subconscious Reprogramming.

Procrastination No More Stop beating yourself up. Use neuroscience to hack your dopamine reward system and trick your brain into taking action effortlessly.

Manifestation (Book 2): Unlocking the Power of the Subconscious Mind Willpower fails; programming sticks. Rewrite the hidden script that says "I am lazy" and replace it with a drive that pulls you forward automatically.

ABOUT THE AUTHOR

Kanav Sachdev

Kanv Sachdev is a modern mystic, author, and teacher dedicated to bridging the gap between ancient Vedic wisdom and contemporary life. With a deep background in the non-dual traditions of Advaita Vedanta and the esoteric practices of Tantra, Kanv's work focuses on demystifying enlightenment and making it accessible to the modern seeker.

He is the author of the In Search of Zero series, including 17 Vedic Meditation Techniques for Inner Stillness and The Mind of Shiva. His writing is known for its blend of high philosophy, practical psychology, and lyrical precision.

Kanv lives in Gurgaon, India, where he writes, teaches, and continues his own Sadhana in the service of the Truth

www.ingramcontent.com/pod-product-compliance
Lightning Source LLC
LaVergne TN
LVHW030911080826
845145LV00010B/2857

9788199751842